FRENCH
in 10 minutes a day®

by Kristine Kershul, M.A., University of California, Santa Barbara

Consultants: Jan Fisher Brousseau   Hagar Shirman
Susan Worthington

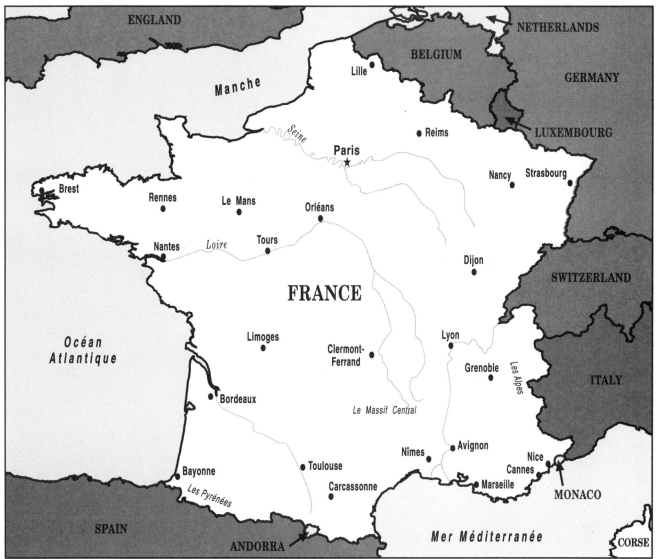

Bilingual Books, Inc.
511 Eastlake Avenue E., Seattle, WA 98109
Tel: (206) 340-4422 Fax: (206) 340-9816
http://www.bilingualbooks.org

Second printing, November 1998

Can you say this?

(kess)   *(kuh)*   *(say)*

Qu'est-ce que c'est?
what is   that

(say)   *(tewn)*   *(fluhr)*

C'est une fleur.
it is   a   flower

(zhuh)   *(voo-dray)*   *(ewn)*   *(fluhr)*

Je voudrais une fleur.
I   would like   a   flower

If you can say this, you can learn to speak French. You will be able to easily order wine, lunch, theater tickets, pastry, or anything else you wish. With your best French accent, you simply ask **"Qu'est-ce que c'est?"** *(kess) (kuh) (say)* and, upon learning what it is, you can order it with **"Je voudrais ça,"** *(zhuh) (voo-dray) (sah)*. Sounds easy, doesn't it?

The purpose of this book is to give you an **immediate** speaking ability in French. French is the leading language not only in France, but in parts of Switzerland, Belgium, Canada and numerous countries in Africa too. French is a language of beautiful sounds. To help you master these sounds, this book offers a unique and easy system of pronunciation above each word which walks you through learning French.

If you are planning a trip or moving to where French is spoken, you will be leaps ahead of everyone if you take just a few minutes a day to learn the easy key words that this book offers. Start with Step 1 and don't skip around. Each day work as far as you can comfortably go in those 10 minutes. Don't overdo it. Some days you might want to just review. If you forget a word, you can always look it up in the glossary. Spend your first 10 minutes studying the map on the previous page. And yes, have fun learning your new language.

As you work through the Steps, always use the special features which only this series offers. This book contains sticky labels and flash cards, free words, puzzles and quizzes. When you have completed this book, cut out the menu guide and take it along on your trip. Do not forget your "Pocket Pal™" which is designed to be carried with you everywhere on your travels and to provide essential backup in case you forget an important word now and then.

(lahl-fah-bay)
L'Alphabet
the alphabet

Throughout this book you will find an an easy pronunciation guide above all new words. Refer to this Step whenever you need help, but remember, spend no longer than 10 minutes a day.

Most letters in French are identical to those in English and are pronounced in just the same way.

(b)	*(d)*	*(f)*	*(k)*	*(l)*	*(m)*	*(n)*	*(p)*	*(t)*	*(v)*	*(z)*
b	**d**	**f**	**k**	**l**	**m**	**n**	**p**	**t**	**v**	**z**

Here is a guide to help you learn the sounds of the French letters which are pronounced somewhat differently. Practice these sounds with the examples given which are mostly towns or areas in France you might wish to visit. You can always refer back to these pages if you need to review.

French letter	English sound	Examples	Write it here
a, à, â	ah	**P**ar**i**s *(pah-ree)*	
ai	ay	**C**al**ai**s *(kah-lay)*	
au, eau	oh	**B**ord**eau**x *(bor-doh)*	
(before a,o,u) **c**	k	**C**olmar *(kohl-mar)*	*Colmar, Colmar, Colmar*
(elsewhere) **c**	s	Ni**c**e *(nees)*	
ç	s	Alen**ç**on *(ah-lah[n]-soh[n])*	
ch	sh	**Ch**ampagne *(shah[n]-pahn-yuh)*	
e	*(as in let)* eh	Montp**e**llier *(moh[n]-pel-yay)*	
	uh	L**e** Havr**e** *(luh)(ah-vruh)*	
è, ê, ei	*(as in let)* eh	la S**ei**ne *(lah)(sen)*	
é	ay	Orl**é**ans *(or-lay-ah[n])*	
(before a,o,u) **g**	g	**G**aronne *(gar-ohn)*	
(before e,i,y) **g**	zh	**G**ironde *(zhee-rohnd)*	
gn	*(as in onion)* n-y	Avi**gn**on *(ah-veen-yoh[n])*	
h	always silent	**H**onfleur *(oh[n]-fluhr)*	
i	ee	L**i**lle *(leel)*	
(before e,i,y) **j**	zh	Le **J**ura *(luh)(zhew-rah)*	
o	oh	Lim**o**ges *(lee-mohzh)*	
oi	wah	P**oi**tiers *(pwah-tee-ay)*	
ou, oû	oo	T**ou**rs *(toor)*	

Letter	Sound	Example	Write it here
qu	k	**Qu**imper *(ka[n]-pair)*	_____
r	r *(slightly rolled)*	**R**ennes *(ren)*	_____
s *(between vowels)*	s	**S**tra**s**bourg *(strahs-boor)*	_____
s	z	Toulou**s**e *(too-looz)*	_____
u	ew/oo *(with your lips rounded)*	Tourn**u**s *(toor-new)*	_____
w	v	Rique**w**ihr *(ree-kuh-veer)*	_____
x	ks	Lu**x**embourg *(lewk-sah[n]-boor)*	_____
	gz	A**x**iat *(ah-gzee-ah)*	_____
	s	Bru**x**elles *(brew-sel)*	_____
y	ee	L**y**on *(lee-oh[n])*	_____

In addition to the sounds above, French has many nasal vowel sounds. Whenever you see the small elevated [n], think nasal!

am, an, em, en	ah[n] *(taunt nasalized)*	**Am**boise *(ah[n]-bwahz)* Ca**en** *(kah-ah[n])*	_____
im, in, aim, ain, eim, ein	a[n] *(than nasalized)*	St.-Sav**in** *(sa[n]-sah-va[n])* S**ain**tes *(sa[n]t)* R**eim**s *(ra[n]s)*	_____
om, on	oh[n] *(don't nasalized)*	Toul**on** *(too-loh[n])*	_____
um, un	uh[n] *(fun nasalized)*	Mel**un** *(mel-uh[n])*	_____
-tion	syoh[n] *(as in station)*	Atten**tion**! *(ah-tah[n]-syoh[n])*	_____

Just as in English, "q" is always joined with the letter "u." The letter "u" is then silent.

Note that when many French words begin with a vowel they are joined together in their pronunciation with the previous word. This liaison is a key part of French pronunciation.

(voo) *(ah-vay)* *(voo)* *(zah-vay)*
vous + **avez** becomes **vous avez**

(say) *(ewn)* *(fluhr)* *(say)* *(tewn)* *(fluhr)*
c'est une fleur becomes **c'est une fleur**

Sometimes the phonetics may seem to contradict your pronunciation guide. Don't panic! The easiest and best possible phonetics have been chosen for each individual word. Pronounce the phonetics just as you see them. Don't over-analyze them. Speak with a French accent and, above all, enjoy yourself!

When you arrive in **France**, *(frah⁽ⁿ⁾s)* **Québec** *(kay-bek)* or another French-speaking country, the very first thing you will need to do is ask questions — "Where (**où**) *(oo)* where is the bus stop?" "**Où** *(oo)* where can I exchange money?" "**Où** is the lavatory?" "**Où** is a restaurant?" "**Où** do I catch a taxi?" "**Où** is a good hotel?" "**Où** is my luggage?" — and the list will go on and on for the entire length of your visit. In French, there are SEVEN KEY QUESTION WORDS to learn. For example, the seven key question words will help you find out exactly what you are ordering in a restaurant before you order it — and not after the surprise (or shock!) arrives. Notice that only one letter is different in the French words for "what" and "who." Don't confuse them! Take a few minutes to study and practice saying the seven key question words listed below. Then cover the French with your hand and fill in each of the blanks with the matching **mot** *(moh)* word **français.** *(frah⁽ⁿ⁾-say)* French

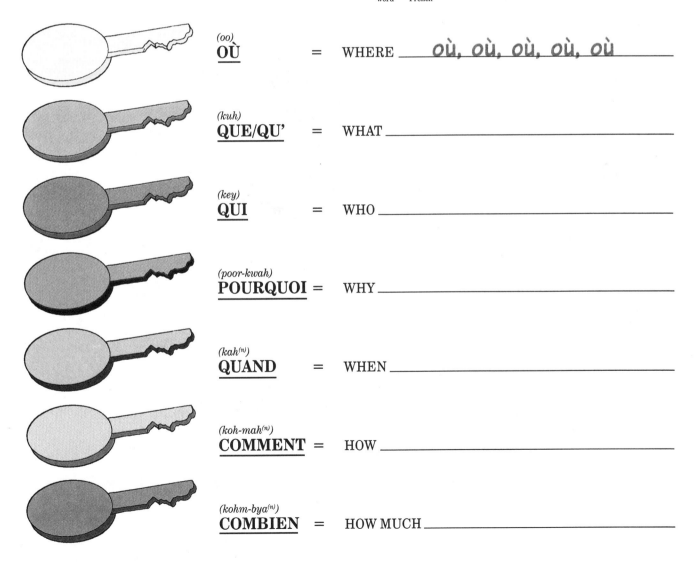

(oo)
OÙ   =   WHERE   *où, où, où, où, où*

(kuh)
QUE/QU'   =   WHAT _____

(key)
QUI   =   WHO _____

(poor-kwah)
POURQUOI =   WHY _____

(kah⁽ⁿ⁾)
QUAND   =   WHEN _____

(koh-mah⁽ⁿ⁾)
COMMENT =   HOW _____

(kohm-bya⁽ⁿ⁾)
COMBIEN =   HOW MUCH _____

5

Now test yourself to see if you really can keep these **mots** *(moh)* words straight in your mind. Draw lines between the French **et** *(ay)* and English equivalents below.

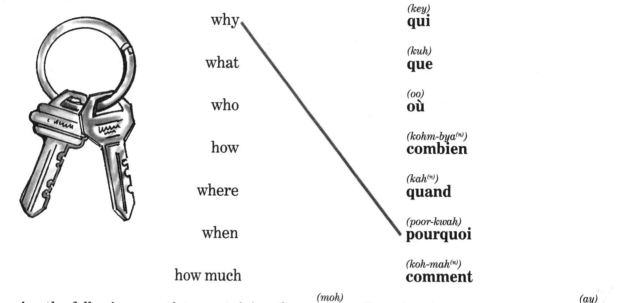

why — **qui** *(key)*

what — **que** *(kuh)*

who — **où** *(oo)*

how — **combien** *(kohm-bya$^{(n)}$)*

where — **quand** *(kah$^{(n)}$)*

when — **pourquoi** *(poor-kwah)*

how much — **comment** *(koh-mah$^{(n)}$)*

Examine the following questions containing these **mots** *(moh)*. Practice the sentences out loud **et** *(ay)* and then practice by copying the French in the blanks underneath each question.

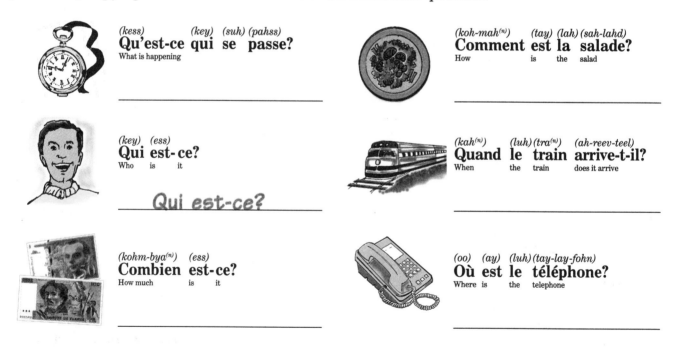

Qu'est-ce qui se passe? *(kess) (key) (suh) (pahss)*
What is happening

_____

Comment est la salade? *(koh-mah$^{(n)}$) (tay) (lah) (sah-lahd)*
How   is   the   salad

_____

Qui est-ce? *(key) (ess)*
Who   is   it

Qui est-ce?

Quand le train arrive-t-il? *(kah$^{(n)}$) (luh) (tra$^{(n)}$) (ah-reev-teel)*
When   the   train   does it arrive

_____

Combien est-ce? *(kohm-bya$^{(n)}$) (ess)*
How much   is   it

_____

Où est le téléphone? *(oo) (ay) (luh) (tay-lay-fohn)*
Where is the   telephone

_____

"**Où**" *(oo)* will be your most used question **mot** *(moh)*. Say each of the following French sentences aloud. Then write out each sentence without looking at the example. If you don't succeed on the first try, don't give up. Just practice each sentence until you are able to do it easily. Remember "**qu**" is pronounced like "k" and "**est-ce**" is pronounced "ess."

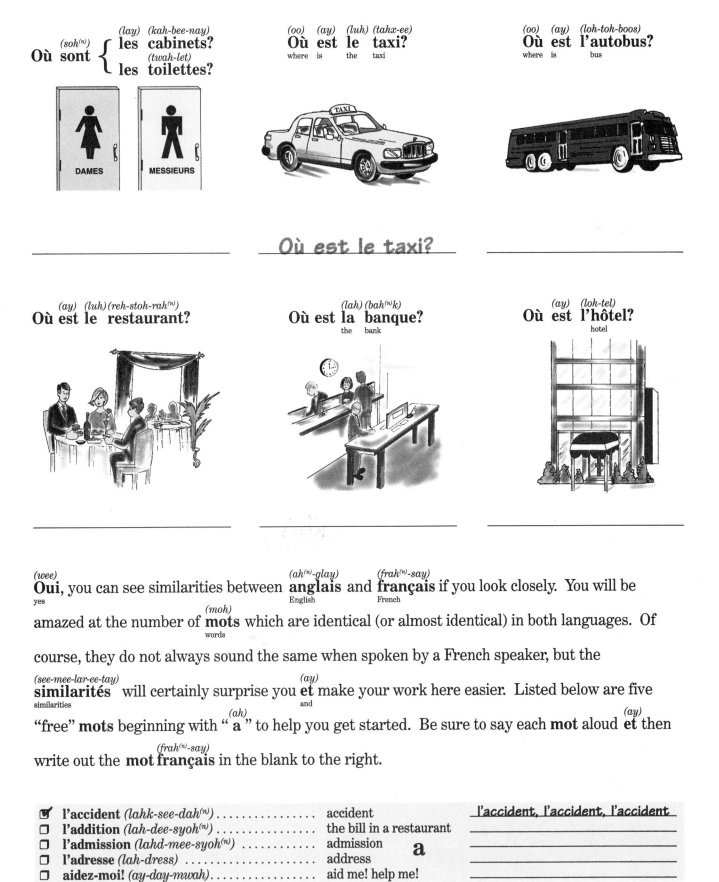

Où sont *(soh⁽ⁿ⁾)* { *(lay)* **les cabinets?** *(kah-bee-nay)*
(twah-let) **les toilettes?**

Où est le taxi?
(oo) (ay) (luh) (tahx-ee)
where is the taxi

Où est l'autobus?
(oo) (ay) (loh-toh-boos)
where is bus

Où est le taxi?

Où est le restaurant?
(ay) (luh) (reh-stoh-rah⁽ⁿ⁾)

Où est la banque?
(lah) (bah⁽ⁿ⁾k)
the bank

Où est l'hôtel?
(ay) (loh-tel)
hotel

Oui, *(wee)* you can see similarities between **anglais** *(ah⁽ⁿ⁾-glay)* and **français** *(frah⁽ⁿ⁾-say)* if you look closely. You will be
yes · English · French

amazed at the number of **mots** *(moh)* which are identical (or almost identical) in both languages. Of
words

course, they do not always sound the same when spoken by a French speaker, but the

similarités *(see-mee-lar-ee-tay)* will certainly surprise you **et** *(ay)* make your work here easier. Listed below are five
similarities · and

"free" **mots** beginning with " **a** *(ah)* " to help you get started. Be sure to say each **mot** aloud **et** *(ay)* then

write out the **mot français** *(frah⁽ⁿ⁾-say)* in the blank to the right.

☑	**l'accident** *(lahk-see-dah⁽ⁿ⁾)*	accident	*l'accident, l'accident, l'accident*
☐	**l'addition** *(lah-dee-syoh⁽ⁿ⁾)*	the bill in a restaurant	_____
☐	**l'admission** *(lahd-mee-syoh⁽ⁿ⁾)*	admission	_____
☐	**l'adresse** *(lah-dress)*	address	_____
☐	**aidez-moi!** *(ay-day-mwah)*	aid me! help me!	_____

a

Free **mots** like these will appear at the bottom of the following pages in a yellow color band.

They are easy — enjoy them! Remember, in French, the letter "**h**" is silent.

3   Odds 'n Ends

(frah⁽ⁿ⁾-say)
Le français has multiple **mots** for "the," "a," and "some," but they are very easy.
French (language)   words

(luh) **le** the	*(lah)* **la** the	*(l)* **l'** the	*(lay)* **les** the	*(uh⁽ⁿ⁾)* **un** a	*(ewn)* **une** a	*(dew)* **du** some	*(duh)(lah)* **de la** some	*(duh)(l)* **de l'** some	*(day)* **des** some

(gar-soh⁽ⁿ⁾)
le garçon
the boy

(gar-soh⁽ⁿ⁾)
les garçons
the boys

(fee-yuh)
la fille
the girl

(fee-yuh)
les filles
the girls

(lohm)
l'homme
the man

(lay) (zohm)
les hommes
the men

(dew) (soo-kruh)
du sucre
some sugar

(duh) (lah) (moo-tard)
de la moutarde
some mustard

(ewn) (fahm)
une femme
a woman

(day) (fahm)
des femmes
some women

(uh) (nohm)
un homme
a man

(day) (zohm)
des hommes
some men

This might appear difficult, but only because it is different from *(ah⁽ⁿ⁾-glay)* **anglais.** Just remember you will be understood whether you say "**la fille** *(fee-yuh)*" or "**le fille**." Soon you will automatically select the right one without even thinking about it.

In Step 2 you were introduced to the Seven Key QuestionWords. These seven words are the basics, the most essential building blocks for learning French. Throughout this book you will come across keys asking you to fill in the missing question word. Use this opportunity not only to fill in the blank on that key, but to review all your question words. Play with the new sounds, speak slowly and have fun.

- ❏ **l'alcool** *(lahl-kohl)* .... alcohol _____
- ❏ **les Alpes** *(lay)(zahlp)* .... the Alps _____
- ❏ **américain** *(ah-may-ree-ka⁽ⁿ⁾)* .... American **a** _____
- ❏ **l'animal** *(lah-nee-mahl)* .... animal _____
- ❏ **l'appartement** *(lah-par-teh-mah⁽ⁿ⁾)* .... apartment _____

Before you proceed **avec** *(ah-vek)* this Step, situate yourself comfortably in your living room. Now look around you. Can you name the things that you see in this **pièce** *(pyess)* in French? You can probably guess **la lampe** *(lahmp)* and maybe even **la chaise** *(shehz).* Let's learn the rest of them. After practicing these **mots** out loud, write them in the blanks below.

la fenêtre *(fuh-net-ruh)*
window

la lampe *(lahmp)* _____ lamp

le canapé *(kah-nah-pay)* _____ sofa

la chaise *(shehz)* _____ chair

le tapis *(tah-pee)* _____ carpet

la table *(tah-bluh)* la table, la table
table

la porte *(port)* _____ door

la pendule *(pah(n)-dewl)* _____ clock

le rideau *(ree-doh)* _____ curtain

le téléphone *(tay-lay-fohn)* _____ telephone

le tableau *(tah-bloh)*
picture

You will notice that the correct form of **le**, **la** or **les** is given **avec** *(ah-vek)* each noun. This tells you whether the noun is masculine (**le**) or feminine (**la**). Now open your book to the sticky labels on page 17 and later on page 35. Peel off the first 11 labels **et** *(ay)* proceed around the **pièce** *(pyess)*, labeling these items in your home. This will help to increase your French **mot** power easily. Don't forget to say each **mot** as you attach the label.

Now ask yourself, **"Où est la lampe?"** *(lahmp)* **et** point at it while you answer, **"Voilà la lampe."** *(vwah-lah)* there is

Continue on down the list above until you feel comfortable with these new **mots.**

□ **l'appétit** *(lah-pay-tee)* .... appetite _____
□ **l'arrêt** *(lah-ray)* .... stop, arrest _____
□ **l'arrivée** *(lah-ree-vay)* .... arrival **a** _____
□ **l'attention** *(lah-tah(n)-syoh(n))* .... attention _____
□ **l'auteur** *(loh-tur)* .... author _____

9

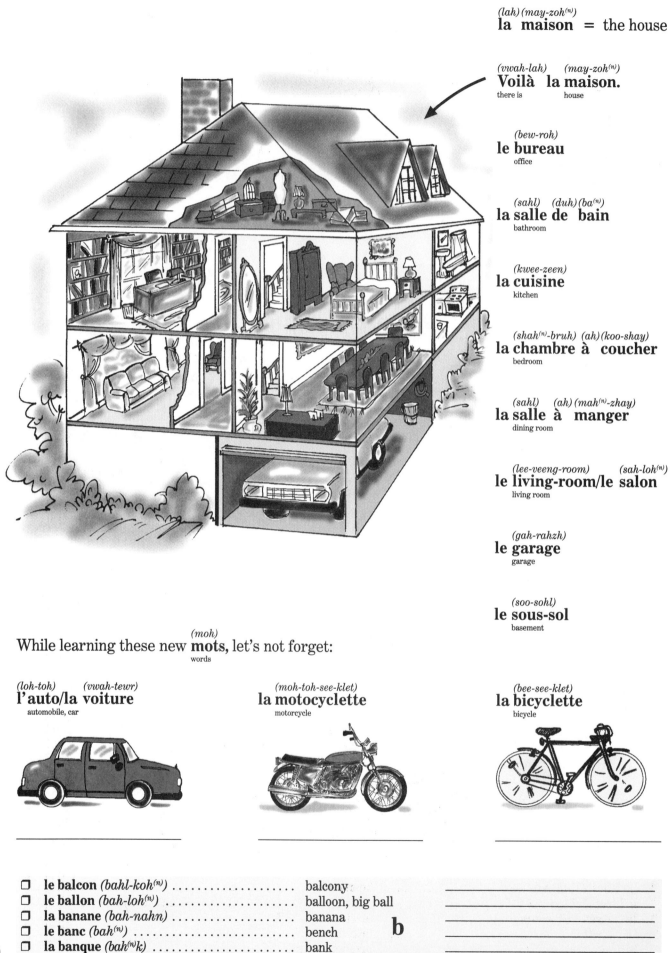

(lah) (may-zoh(n))
la maison = the house

(vwah-lah)   (may-zoh(n))
Voilà la maison.
there is   house

(bew-roh)
le bureau
office

(sahl)   (duh) (ba(n))
la salle de bain
bathroom

(kwee-zeen)
la cuisine
kitchen

(shah(n)-bruh) (ah)(koo-shay)
la chambre à coucher
bedroom

(sahl)   (ah) (mah(n)-zhay)
la salle à manger
dining room

(lee-veeng-room)   (sah-loh(n))
le living-room/le salon
living room

(gah-rahzh)
le garage
garage

(soo-sohl)
le sous-sol
basement

(moh)
While learning these new **mots,** let's not forget:
words

(loh-toh)   (vwah-tewr)
l'auto/la voiture
automobile, car

(moh-toh-see-klet)
la motocyclette
motorcycle

(bee-see-klet)
la bicyclette
bicycle

☐ **le balcon** *(bahl-koh(n))*	balcony	
☐ **le ballon** *(bah-loh(n))*	balloon, big ball	
☐ **la banane** *(bah-nahn)*	banana	**b**
☐ **le banc** *(bah(n))*	bench	
☐ **la banque** *(bah(n)k)*	bank	

(shah)
le chat
cat

(zhar-da$^{(n)}$)
le jardin
garden

(fluhr)
les fleurs
flowers

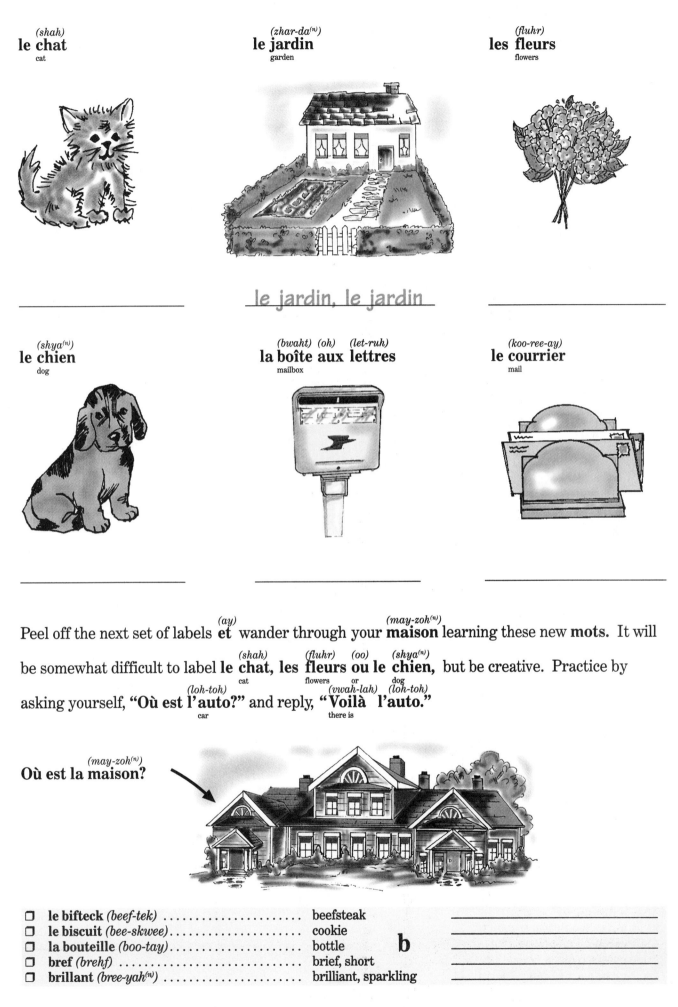

le jardin, le jardin

(shya$^{(n)}$)
le chien
dog

(bwaht) (oh) (let-ruh)
la boîte aux lettres
mailbox

(koo-ree-ay)
le courrier
mail

Peel off the next set of labels **et** *(ay)* wander through your **maison** *(may-zoh$^{(n)}$)* learning these new **mots**. It will be somewhat difficult to label **le chat**, *(shah)* cat **les fleurs** *(fluhr)* flowers **ou** *(oo)* or **le chien,** *(shya$^{(n)}$)* dog but be creative. Practice by asking yourself, **"Où est l'auto?"** *(loh-toh)* car and reply, **"Voilà** *(vwah-lah)* there is **l'auto."** *(loh-toh)*

Où est la maison? *(may-zoh$^{(n)}$)*

☐ **le bifteck** *(beef-tek)* . . . . beefsteak
☐ **le biscuit** *(bee-skwee)* . . . . cookie
☐ **la bouteille** *(boo-tay)* . . . . bottle
☐ **bref** *(brehf)* . . . . brief, short
☐ **brillant** *(bree-yah$^{(n)}$)* . . . . brilliant, sparkling

b

(uh⁽ⁿ⁾) *(duh)* *(twah)*
Un, Deux, Trois!
one   two   three

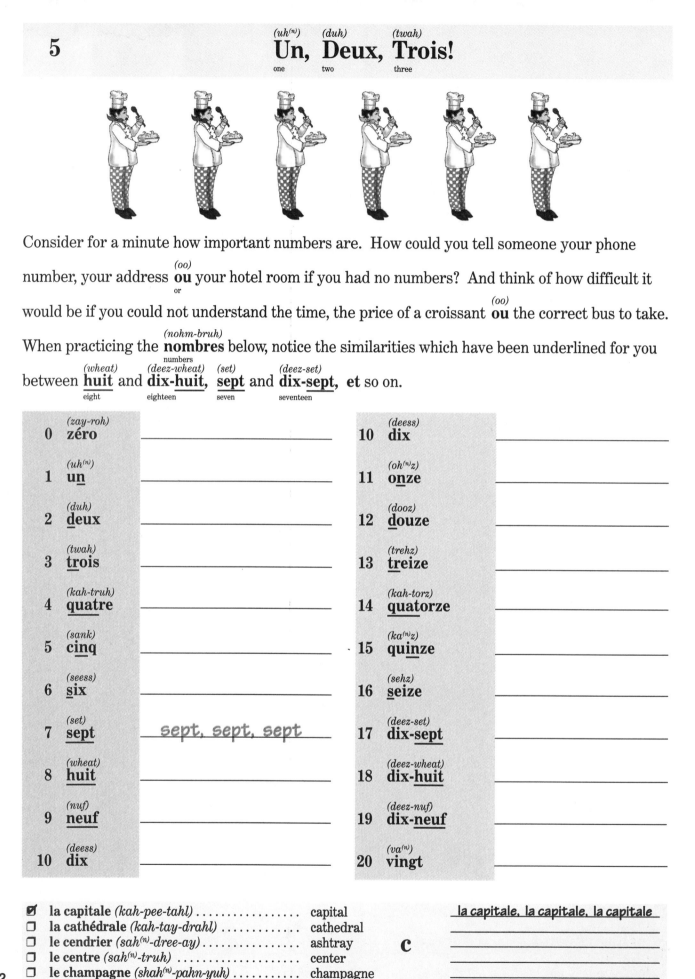

Consider for a minute how important numbers are. How could you tell someone your phone

number, your address **ou** *(oo)* or your hotel room if you had no numbers? And think of how difficult it

would be if you could not understand the time, the price of a croissant **ou** *(oo)* the correct bus to take.

When practicing the **nombres** *(nohm-bruh)* numbers below, notice the similarities which have been underlined for you

between **huit** *(wheat)* eight and **dix-huit,** *(deez-wheat)* eighteen **sept** *(set)* seven and **dix-sept,** *(deez-set)* seventeen **et** so on.

0	*(zay-roh)* **zéro**	_____	10	*(deess)* **dix**	_____
1	*(uh⁽ⁿ⁾)* **un**	_____	11	*(oh⁽ⁿ⁾z)* **onze**	_____
2	*(duh)* **deux**	_____	12	*(dooz)* **douze**	_____
3	*(twah)* **trois**	_____	13	*(trehz)* **treize**	_____
4	*(kah-truh)* **quatre**	_____	14	*(kah-torz)* **quatorze**	_____
5	*(sank)* **cinq**	_____	15	*(ka⁽ⁿ⁾z)* **quinze**	_____
6	*(seess)* **six**	_____	16	*(sehz)* **seize**	_____
7	*(set)* **sept**	*sept, sept, sept*	17	*(deez-set)* **dix-sept**	_____
8	*(wheat)* **huit**	_____	18	*(deez-wheat)* **dix-huit**	_____
9	*(nuf)* **neuf**	_____	19	*(deez-nuf)* **dix-neuf**	_____
10	*(deess)* **dix**	_____	20	*(va⁽ⁿ⁾)* **vingt**	_____

☑	**la capitale** *(kah-pee-tahl)*	capital	*la capitale, la capitale, la capitale*
☐	**la cathédrale** *(kah-tay-drahl)*	cathedral	_____
☐	**le cendrier** *(sah⁽ⁿ⁾-dree-ay)*	ashtray	**c** _____
☐	**le centre** *(sah⁽ⁿ⁾-truh)*	center	_____
☐	**le champagne** *(shah⁽ⁿ⁾-pahn-yuh)*	champagne	_____

(ew-tee-lee-zay) *(nohm-bruh)* *(ah(n))*
Utilisez these **nombres** on a daily basis. Count to yourself **en français** when you brush your
use   numbers   in   French

(oo) *(nohm-bruh)*
teeth, exercise **ou** commute to work. Fill in the blanks below according to the **nombres** given in
                  or   numbers

parentheses. Now is also a good time to learn these two very important phrases.

(zhuh) *(voo-dray)*
je voudrais _____
I   would like

(noo) *(voo-dree-oh(n))*
nous voudrions _____
we   would like

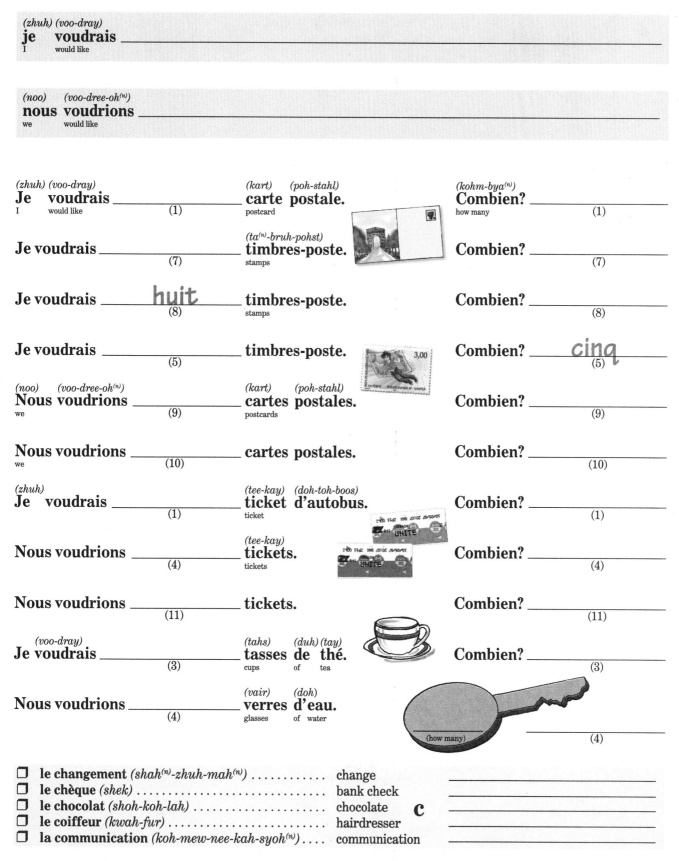

(zhuh) *(voo-dray)*
Je voudrais _____ carte postale.
I   would like (1)   postcard

(kart) *(poh-stahl)*
carte postale.
postcard

(kohm-bya(n))
Combien? _____
how many (1)

Je voudrais _____ timbres-poste.
(7)

(ta(n)-bruh-pohst)
timbres-poste.
stamps

Combien? _____
(7)

Je voudrais ___huit___ timbres-poste.
(8)   stamps

Combien? _____
(8)

Je voudrais _____ timbres-poste.
(5)

Combien? ___cinq___
(5)

(noo) *(voo-dree-oh(n))*
Nous voudrions _____ cartes postales.
we (9)   postcards

(kart) *(poh-stahl)*
cartes postales.

Combien? _____
(9)

Nous voudrions _____ cartes postales.
we (10)

Combien? _____
(10)

(zhuh)
Je voudrais _____ ticket d'autobus.
(1)

(tee-kay) *(doh-toh-boos)*
ticket d'autobus.
ticket

Combien? _____
(1)

Nous voudrions _____ tickets.
(4)

(tee-kay)
tickets.
tickets

Combien? _____
(4)

Nous voudrions _____ tickets.
(11)

Combien? _____
(11)

(voo-dray)
Je voudrais _____ tasses de thé.
(3)

(tahs) *(duh)* *(tay)*
tasses de thé.
cups   of   tea

Combien? _____
(3)

Nous voudrions _____ verres d'eau.
(4)

(vair) *(doh)*
verres d'eau.
glasses   of water

_____
(how many)

_____
(4)

☐ **le changement** *(shah(n)-zhuh-mah(n))* .... change   _____
☐ **le chèque** *(shek)* .... bank check   _____
☐ **le chocolat** *(shoh-koh-lah)* .... chocolate   **c**   _____
☐ **le coiffeur** *(kwah-fur)* .... hairdresser   _____
☐ **la communication** *(koh-mew-nee-kah-syoh(n))* .... communication   _____

Now see if you can translate the following thoughts into **français.** **Les réponses** are provided
(lay) *(ray-poh⁽ⁿ⁾s)*
French   answers

upside down at the bottom of the **page.**
(pahzh)
page

1. I would like seven postcards.

    _____

2. I would like nine stamps.

    _____

3. We would like four cups of tea.

    _____

4. We would like three bus tickets.

    _____

Review **les nombres** 1 à $\overset{(ah)}{}$ 20. Write out your telephone number, fax number **et** $\overset{(ay)}{}$ cellular number.

Then write out a friend's telephone number and a relative's telephone number.

| (2 | 0 | 6) | 3 | 4 | 0 | — | 4 | 4 | 2 | 2 |

deux zéro six _____

(   )   __ __ __ — __ __ __ __

_____

(   )   __ __ __ — __ __ __ __

_____

6

(lay) *(koo-luhr)*
Les Couleurs
colors

(koo-luhr) *(soh⁽ⁿ⁾)* *(ah⁽ⁿ⁾)(frah⁽ⁿ⁾s)* *(oh)* *(kay-bek)*
Les couleurs sont the same **en France et au Québec** as they are in the United States — they just
colors   are   in   in

(noh⁽ⁿ⁾) *(vee-oh-lay)* *(bluh)*
have different **noms**. You can easily recognize **violet** as violet and **bleu** as blue. Let's learn the
names

(koo-luhr) *(may-zoh⁽ⁿ⁾)*
basic **couleurs** so when you are invited to someone's **maison et** you want to bring flowers, you
house

(koo-luhr)
will be able to order the color you want. Once you've learned **les couleurs,** quiz yourself. What

color are your shoes? Your eyes? Your hair? Your house?

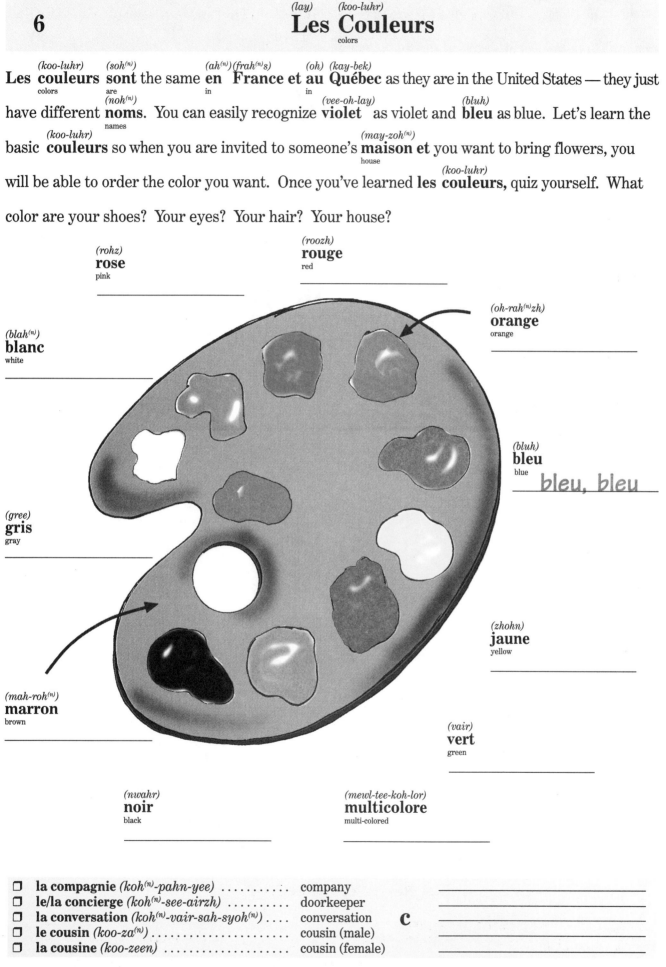

(rohz)
rose
pink

(roozh)
rouge
red

(oh-rah⁽ⁿ⁾zh)
orange
orange

(blah⁽ⁿ⁾)
blanc
white

(bluh)
bleu
blue   *bleu, bleu*

(gree)
gris
gray

(mah-roh⁽ⁿ⁾)
marron
brown

(zhohn)
jaune
yellow

(vair)
vert
green

(nwahr)
noir
black

(mewl-tee-koh-lor)
multicolore
multi-colored

❏	**la compagnie** *(koh⁽ⁿ⁾-pahn-yee)*	company	
❏	**le/la concierge** *(koh⁽ⁿ⁾-see-airzh)*	doorkeeper	
❏	**la conversation** *(koh⁽ⁿ⁾-vair-sah-syoh⁽ⁿ⁾)*	conversation	**c**
❏	**le cousin** *(koo-za⁽ⁿ⁾)*	cousin (male)	
❏	**la cousine** *(koo-zeen)*	cousin (female)	

Peel off the next group of labels **et** proceed to label these **couleurs** *(koo-luhr)* in your **maison.** *(may-zoh(n))* house Identify the

two **ou** *(oo)* or three dominant colors in the flags below.

Algeria	_____	Belgium	_____
Cameroon	_____	Canada	_____
Chad	_____	France	_____
French Guiana	_____	Haiti	_____
Ivory Coast	_____	Luxembourg	_____
Madagascar	_____	Mali	_____
Monaco	_____	Switzerland	_____

You should be able to use your **français** *(frah(n)-say)* language skills in any of the above countries as well as in

France.

_____ _____ est le **taxi?** *(tahx-ee)*
(where)   (where)

_____ _____ ?
(what)   (what is that)

☐ **la dame** *(dahm)*	lady	_____
☐ **la danse** *(dah(n)s)*	dance	_____
☐ **décembre** *(day-sah(n)m-bruh)*	December	**d** _____
☐ **la déclaration** *(day-klah-rah-syoh(n))*	declaration	_____
☐ **le départ** *(day-par)*	departure	_____

(lahmp)	(loh-toh)	(mah-roh(n))	(bee-air)
la **lampe**	l'**auto**	**marron**	la **bière**

(kah-nah-pay)
le **canapé**

(moh-toh-see-klet)
la **motocyclette**

(roozh)
rouge

(lay)
le **lait**

(shehz)
la **chaise**

(bee-see-klet)
la **bicyclette**

(rohz)
rose

(buhr)
le **beurre**

(tah-pee)
le **tapis**

(shah)
le **chat**

(oh-rah(n)zh)
orange

(sel)
le **sel**

(zhar-da(n))
le **jardin**

(blah(n))
blanc

(pwah-vruh)
le **poivre**

(fluhr)
les **fleurs**

(zhohn)
jaune

(vair) (va(n))
le **verre à vin**

(shya(n))
le **chien**

(gree)
gris

(vair)
le **verre**

(ree-doh)
le **rideau**

(bwaht) (oh) (let-ruh)
la **boîte aux lettres**

(nwahr)
noir

(zhoor-nahl)
le **journal**

(tay-lay-fohn)
le **téléphone**

(koo-ree-ay)
le **courrier**

(bluh)
bleu

(tahs)
la **tasse**

(fuh-net-ruh)
la **fenêtre**

0 (zay-roh) **zéro**

(vair)
vert

(kwee-air)
la **cuillère**

(tah-bloh)
le **tableau**

1 (uh(n)) **un**

(mewl-tee-koh-lor)
multicolore

(koo-toh)
le **couteau**

(may-zoh(n))
la **maison**

2 (duh) **deux**

(boh(n)-zhoor)
bonjour

(sair-vyet)
la **serviette**

(bew-roh)
le **bureau**

3 (twah) **trois**

(boh(n)-swahr)
bonsoir

(lah-syet)
l'**assiette**

(sahl) (ba(n))
salle de bain

4 (kah-truh) **quatre**

(bun) (nwee)
bonne nuit

(foor-shet)
la **fourchette**

(kwee-zeen)
la **cuisine**

5 (sank) **cinq**

(sah-lew)
salut

(plah-kar)
le **placard**

(shah(n)-bruh) (koo-shay)
chambre à coucher

6 (seess) **six**

(oh) (ruh-vwahr)
au revoir

(tay)
le **thé**

(sahl) (mah(n)-zhay)
salle à manger

7 (set) **sept**

(koh-mah(n)) (tah-lay-voo)
Comment allez-vous?

(lee-veeng-room)
living-room

8 (wheat) **huit**

(pa(n))
le **pain**

(gah-rahzh)
le **garage**

9 (nuf) **neuf**

(kwee-zeen-yair)
le **cuisinière**

(seel) (voo) (play)
s'il vous plaît

(soo-sohl)
le **sous-sol**

10 (deess) **dix**

(mair-see)
merci

STICKY LABELS

This book has over 150 special sticky labels for you to use as you learn new words. When you are introduced to one of these words, remove the corresponding label from these pages. Be sure to use each of these unique self-adhesive labels by adhering them to a picture, window, lamp, or whatever object they refer to. And yes, they are removable! The sticky labels make learning to speak French much more fun and a lot easier than you ever expected. For example, when you look in the mirror and see the label, say

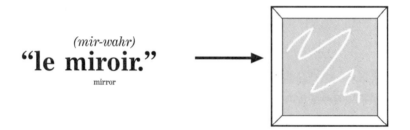

(mir-wahr)
"le miroir."
mirror

Don't just say it once, say it again and again. And once you label the refrigerator, you should never again open that door without saying

(ray-free-zhay-rah-tuhr)
"le réfrigérateur."
refrigerator

By using the sticky labels, you not only learn new words, but friends and family learn along with you! The sooner you start, the sooner you can use these labels at home or work.

Before starting this Step, go back and review Step 5. It is important that you can count to

(va⁽ⁿ⁾)
vingt without looking at **le livre.** *(lee-vruh)* Let's learn the larger **nombres** *(nohm-bruh)* now. After practicing aloud
twenty   book

(lay)   *(frah⁽ⁿ⁾-say)*
les nombres français 10 through 1,000 below, write these **nombres** in the blanks provided.

Again, notice the similarities (underlined) between **nombres** such as **quatre** (4) *(kah-truh)*, **quatorze** (14) *(kah-torz)*,

(kah-rah⁽ⁿ⁾t)
et quarante (40).

10	*(deess)* **dix**	
20	*(va⁽ⁿ⁾)* **vingt**	
30	*(trah⁽ⁿ⁾t)* **trente**	
40	*(kah-rah⁽ⁿ⁾t)* **quarante**	*quarante, quarante, quarante, quarante, quarante*
50	*(sang-kah⁽ⁿ⁾t)* **cinquante**	
60	*(swah-sah⁽ⁿ⁾t)* **soixante**	
70	*(swah-sah⁽ⁿ⁾t-deess)* **soixante-dix** (60+10)	
80	*(kah-truh-va⁽ⁿ⁾)* **quatre-vingts** (4 x 20)	
90	*(kah-truh-va⁽ⁿ⁾-deess)* **quatre-vingt-dix** (4 x 20+10)	
100	*(sah⁽ⁿ⁾)* **cent**	
500	*(sank) (sah⁽ⁿ⁾)* **cinq cents**	
1,000	*(meel)* **mille**	

(duh)
Here are **deux** important phrases to go with all these **nombres.** Say them out loud over and over

and then write them out twice as many times.

(zhay)
j'ai _____
I have

(noo) (zah-voh⁽ⁿ⁾)
nous avons _____
we   have

❏ **déjà** *(day-zhah)*	already	_____
– **déjà vu** *(day-zhah)(vew)*	already seen	_____
❏ **la désir** *(day-zeer)*	desire	_____
❏ **la distance** *(dee-stah⁽ⁿ⁾s)*	distance	_____
❏ **le docteur** *(dohk-tur)*	doctor	_____

d

The unit of currency **en France** *(ay)* **est le franc français,** *(frah(n))(frah(n)-say)* abbreviated "**F**". Let's learn the various
in   is

kinds of **monnaie et billets.** *(moh-nay)(bee-ay)* Always be sure to practice each **mot** *(moh)* out loud. You might want to
coins   bills

exchange some money **maintenant** *(ma(n)-tuh-nah(n))* so that you can familiarize yourself **avec** *(ah-vek)* the various types of
now   with

argent. *(ar-zhah(n))*
money

Billets *(bee-ay)*
bills

cinquante francs *(sang-kah(n)t)*
50

cent francs *(sah(n))*
100

deux cent francs *(sah(n))*
200

cinq cents *(sank)(sah(n))*
500

francs

Monnaie *(moh-nay)*
coins

dix centimes *(dee)(sah(n)-teem)*
ten

vingt centimes *(va(n))*

cinquante centimes *(sang-kah(n)t)*
50

un franc *(uh(n))(frah(n))*

deux francs *(duh)(frah(n))*

cinq francs *(sank)*

dix francs *(deess)*

☐ **l'économie** *(lay-koh-noh-mee)* .... economy _____
☐ **l'entrée** *(lah(n)-tray)* .... entry, entrance _____
☐ **est** *(est)* .... east **e** _____
☐ **l'état** *(lay-tah)* .... state _____
– **Les États-Unis** *(lay)(zay-tah-zoo-nee)* The United States of America _____

20

Review **les nombres dix** (*deess*) through **mille** (*meel*) again. **Maintenant,** (*ma⁽ⁿ⁾-tuh-nah⁽ⁿ⁾*) how do you say "twenty-two" **ou** (*oo*)
now

"fifty-three" **en français?** (*ah⁽ⁿ⁾*) Put the numbers together in a logical sequence just as you do in

English. See if you can say **et** write out **les nombres** on this **page.** (*pahzh*) The answers **sont** (*soh⁽ⁿ⁾*) at the
page   are

bottom of **la page**.

1. _____   2. _____
          (25 = 20 + 5)   (83 = 80 + 3)

3. _____   4. ___quatre-vingt-seize___
          (47 = 40 + 7)   (96 = 90 + 6)

Now, how would you say the following **en français?** (*frah⁽ⁿ⁾-say*)

5. _____
                    (I have 80 francs.)

6. _____
                    (We have 72 francs.)

To ask how much something costs **en français,** one asks — **Combien** (*kohm-bya⁽ⁿ⁾*) **est-ce** (*ess*) **que** (*kuh*) **ça** (*sah*) **coûte?** (*koot*)

Now you try it. _____
                              (How much does that cost?)

Answer the following questions based on the numbers in parentheses.

7. **Combien** (*kohm-bya⁽ⁿ⁾*) **est-ce** (*ess*) **que** (*kuh*) **ça** (*sah*) **coûte?** (*koot*) **Ça coûte** _____ francs.
   costs   this   it costs   (10)

8. **Combien coûte** (*koot*) **le ticket?** (*tee-kay*) **Le ticket coûte** _____ francs.
              costs   (20)

9. **Combien coûte le livre?** (*lee-vruh*) **Le livre coûte** _____ francs.
                    book   (17)

10. **Combien coûte le film?** (*feelm*) **Le film coûte** _____ francs.
                                                           (30)

RÉPONSES

10. **trente**	5. **J'ai quatre-vingt francs.**
9. **dix-sept**	4. **quatre-vingt-seize**
8. **vingt**	3. **quarante-sept**
7. **dix**	2. **quatre-vingt-trois**
6. **Nous avons soixante-douze francs.**	1. **vingt-cinq**

21

8

(oh-zhoor-dwee)
Aujourd'hui, *(duh-ma⁽ⁿ⁾)* **Demain** et *(ee-air)* **Hier**
today   tomorrow   and   yesterday

(kah-lah⁽ⁿ⁾-dree-ay)
Le calendrier
calendar

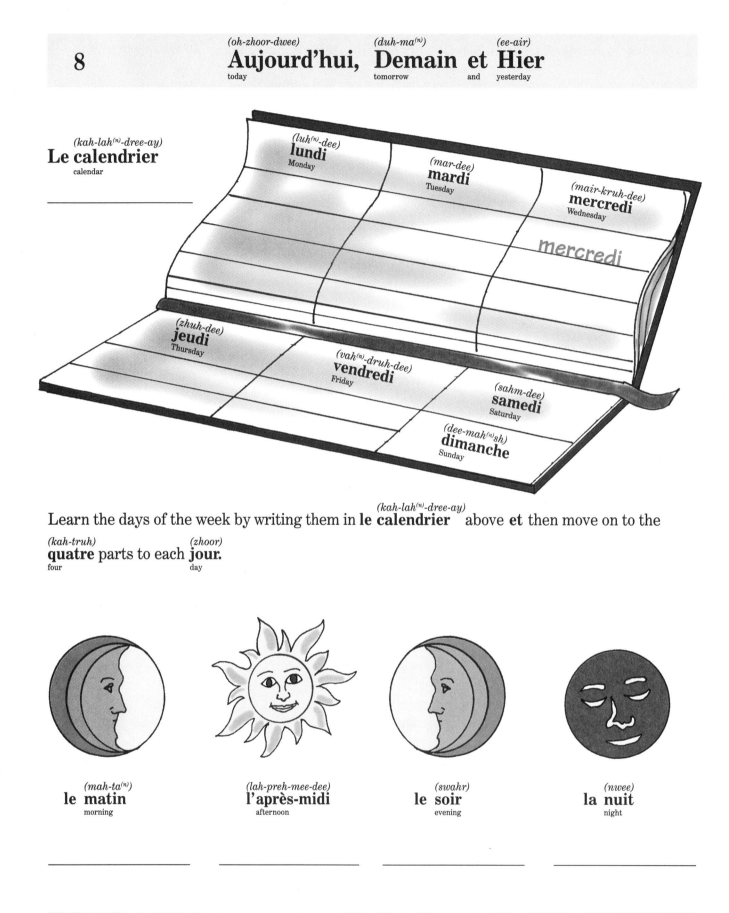

(luh⁽ⁿ⁾-dee)
lundi
Monday

(mar-dee)
mardi
Tuesday

(mair-kruh-dee)
mercredi
Wednesday

mercredi

(zhuh-dee)
jeudi
Thursday

(vah⁽ⁿ⁾-druh-dee)
vendredi
Friday

(sahm-dee)
samedi
Saturday

(dee-mah⁽ⁿ⁾sh)
dimanche
Sunday

Learn the days of the week by writing them in **le calendrier** *(kah-lah⁽ⁿ⁾-dree-ay)* above **et** then move on to the

(kah-truh) *(zhoor)*
quatre parts to each **jour.**
four   day

(mah-ta⁽ⁿ⁾)
le **matin**
morning

(lah-preh-mee-dee)
l'**après-midi**
afternoon

(swahr)
le **soir**
evening

(nwee)
la **nuit**
night

_____ _____ _____ _____

☐ **la fatigue** *(fah-teeg)*	fatigue, tiredness	_____
– **je suis fatigué** *(zhuh)(swee)(fah-tee-gay)* . .	I am tired	_____
☐ **la fête** *(fet)*	feast, festival **f**	_____
☐ **le festival** *(feh-stee-vahl)*	festival	_____
☐ **le film** *(feelm)*	film	_____

Il est très important to know the days of the week **et** the various parts of the day as well as these **trois mots.**

(eel)(ay) (treh) (za^{(n)}-por-tah^{(n)})
very   important

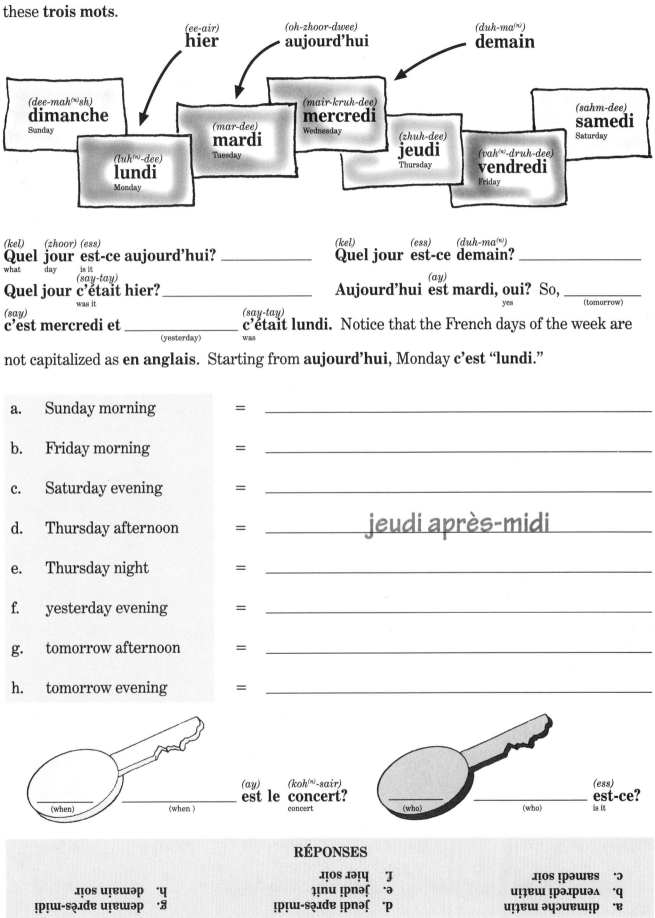

(ee-air) **hier**

(oh-zhoor-dwee) **aujourd'hui**

(duh-ma^{(n)}) **demain**

(dee-mah^{(n)}sh) **dimanche** Sunday

(luh^{(n)}-dee) **lundi** Monday

(mar-dee) **mardi** Tuesday

(mair-kruh-dee) **mercredi** Wednesday

(zhuh-dee) **jeudi** Thursday

(vah^{(n)}-druh-dee) **vendredi** Friday

(sahm-dee) **samedi** Saturday

(kel) (zhoor) (ess)
Quel jour est-ce aujourd'hui? _____
what   day   is it

(say-tay)
Quel jour c'était hier? _____
was it

(say)
c'est mercredi et _____ **c'était lundi.** Notice that the French days of the week are (yesterday)   was

(kel) (ess) (duh-ma^{(n)})
Quel jour est-ce demain? _____

(ay)
Aujourd'hui est mardi, oui? So, _____
yes   (tomorrow)

(say-tay)

not capitalized as **en anglais.** Starting from **aujourd'hui,** Monday **c'est "lundi."**

a.	Sunday morning	=	_____
b.	Friday morning	=	_____
c.	Saturday evening	=	_____
d.	Thursday afternoon	=	*jeudi après-midi*
e.	Thursday night	=	_____
f.	yesterday evening	=	_____
g.	tomorrow afternoon	=	_____
h.	tomorrow evening	=	_____

_____ _____ **est le concert?**
(when)   (when)

(ay) (koh^{(n)}-sair)
concert

_____ _____ **est-ce?**
(who)   (who)

(ess)
is it

23

Knowing the parts of **le jour** will help you to learn the various **salutations** *(sah-lew-tah-syoh[n])* **françaises** *(frah[n]-sez)* below.
day   greetings

Practice these every day until your trip.

(boh[n]-zhoor)
bonjour _____
good morning/good day

(boh[n]-swahr)
bonsoir _____
good evening

(bun) *(nwee)*
bonne nuit _____
good   night

(sah-lew)
salut _____
hello/hi

(oh) *(ruh-vwahr)*
au revoir _____
goodbye

Take the next **quatre** labels **et** stick them on the appropriate **choses** *(shohz)* in your **maison.** *(may-zoh[n])* Make sure
four   things   house

you attach them to the correct items, as they are only **en français.** *(ah[n])* How about the bathroom

mirror **pour** *(poor)* "bonjour"? **Ou** *(oo)* your alarm clock for **"bonne** *(bun)* **nuit"?** *(nwee)* Let's not forget,
for   or

(koh-mah[n]) *(tah-lay-voo)*
Comment allez-vous? _____
how are you

Now for some **"oui"** *(wee)* or **"non"** *(noh[n])* questions –
yes   no

(bluh)
Are your eyes **bleus?** _____

Are your shoes **marrons?** *(mah-roh[n])* _____

(roozh)
Is your favorite color **rouge?** _____

Is today **samedi?** _____

(shya[n])
Do you own a **chien?** _____

(shah)
Do you own a **chat?** _____

You **êtes** *(et)* about one-fourth of your way through this **livre** *(lee-vruh)* **et c'est** *(say)* a good time to quickly review
are   book   it is

les mots you have learned before doing the crossword puzzle on the next **page.** **Amusez-vous** *(ah-mew-zay-voo)*
enjoy yourself

et bonne *(bun)* **chance!** *(shah[n]s)*
good   luck

CROSSWORD PUZZLE (MOTS CROISÉS) *(kwah-zay)*

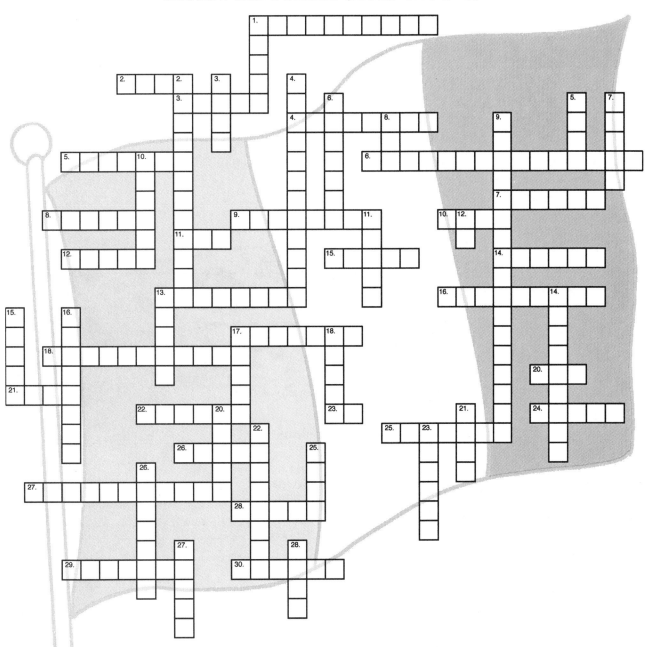

ACROSS

1. I would like
2. with
3. (we) have
4. America
5. coins
6. bus ticket
7. Saturday
8. bank
9. 19
10. night
11. tea
12. 20
13. Wednesday
14. chair
15. man
16. 50
17. clock
18. today
20. water
21. five
22. four
23. and
24. there is
25. how?
26. yellow
27. multi-colored
28. three
29. picture
30. curtain

DOWN

1. days
2. postcard
3. black
4. the afternoon
5. car
6. response, answer
7. hi
8. who?
9. what is it?
10. money
11. woman
12. a (masculine)
13. Tuesday
14. we have
15. white
16. why?
17. room
18. lamp
20. red
21. green
22. Friday
23. house
25. gray
26. how much?
27. when?
28. two

❏ **le filtre** *(feel-truh)* . . . . filter
  – un café filtre *(kah-fay)(feel-truh)* . . . . filtered coffee   **f** _____
❏ **la fin** *(fa⁽ⁿ⁾)* . . . . end   _____
❏ **le fonctionnaire** *(foh⁽ⁿ⁾-syoh-nair)* . . . . functionary, civil servant _____
❏ **le football** *(foot-bahl)* . . . . soccer

(dah⁽ⁿ⁾) *(sewr)* *(soo)*
Dans, sur, sous...
in   on   under

(pray-poh-zee-syoh⁽ⁿ⁾) *(frah⁽ⁿ⁾-sez)*
Les prépositions françaises (words like "in," "on," "through" and "next to") **sont** easy to

(are)

learn, **et** they allow you to be precise **avec** a minimum of effort. Instead of having to point **six** *(seess)*

times **at** a piece of yummy pastry you would like, you can explain precisely which one you want

(eel)
by saying **il est** behind, in front of, next to **ou** under the piece of pastry that the salesperson is

it is

(puh-tee)
starting to pick up. Let's learn some of these **petits mots.**

little

(soo)
sous _____
under

(dah⁽ⁿ⁾)
dans _____
into/in

(oh-duh-syoo) *(duh)*
au-dessus de* _____
over

(duh-vah⁽ⁿ⁾)
devant _____
in front of

(ah⁽ⁿ⁾-truh)
entre ___ *entre, entre, entre* ___
between

(dair-ee-air)
derrière _____
behind

(ah) (koh-tay) (duh)
à côté de* _____
next to

(duh)
de* _____
out of/from

(sewr)
sur _____
on

(pah-tee-suh-ree)
la pâtisserie _____
pastry!

***Note that "de"** sometimes combines with "**la**," "**le**" or "**les**" to form "**de la,**" "**du,**" *(de+le)* "**de l'**" and

(de+les)
"**des.**" Fill in the blanks on the next **page** with the correct prepositions.

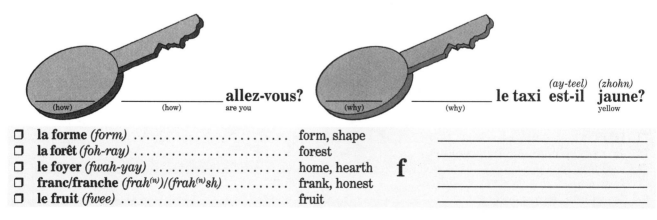

_____ **allez-vous?**
(how)   (how)   are you

_____ **le taxi est-il jaune?**
(why)   (why)   *(ay-teel)* *(zhohn)*
yellow

☐ **la forme** *(form)* .... form, shape
☐ **la forêt** *(foh-ray)* .... forest
☐ **le foyer** *(fwah-yay)* .... home, hearth   **f**
☐ **franc/franche** *(frah⁽ⁿ⁾)/(frah⁽ⁿ⁾sh)* .... frank, honest
☐ **le fruit** *(fwee)* .... fruit

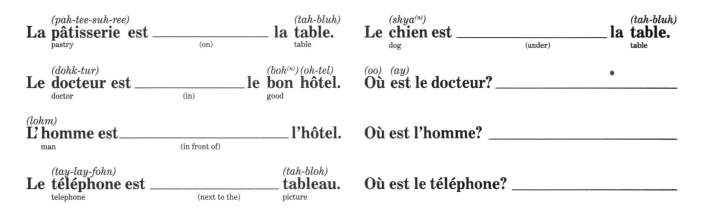

(pah-tee-suh-ree)
La pâtisserie est _____ *(tah-bluh)* **la table.**
pastry   (on)   table

(shya⁽ⁿ⁾)
Le chien est _____ *(tah-bluh)* **la table.**
dog   (under)   table

(dohk-tur)
Le docteur est _____ *(boh⁽ⁿ⁾) (oh-tel)* **le bon hôtel.**
doctor   (in)   good

(oo) (ay)
Où est le docteur? _____

(lohm)
L' homme est _____ **l'hôtel.**
man   (in front of)

Où est l'homme? _____

(tay-lay-fohn)
Le téléphone est _____ *(tah-bloh)* **tableau.**
telephone   (next to the)   picture

Où est le téléphone? _____

(ma⁽ⁿ⁾-tuh-nah⁽ⁿ⁾)
Maintenant, fill in each blank on the picture below with the best possible one of these *(puh-tee)* **petits**
now   little

mots. Do you recognize **la** *(kah-tay-drahl)* **Cathédrale** *(noh-truh-dahm)* **Notre-Dame** below?

(over)

(between)

(next to)

(behind)

(in, into)

(under)

(in front of)

❐	**la galerie** *(gah-leh-ree)*	gallery, long room	_____
❐	**la géographie** *(zhay-oh-grah-fee)*	geography	_____
❐	**la glace** *(glahs)*	ice, ice cream **g**	_____
❐	**la gomme** *(gohm)*	eraser	_____
❐	**le gourmand** *(goor-mah⁽ⁿ⁾)*	gourmand, glutton	_____

(zhah⁽ⁿ⁾-vee-ay) *(fay-vree-ay)* *(marss)*
Janvier, Février, Mars
January   February   March

You have learned the days of **la semaine,** *(suh-men)* week, so now **c'est le** *(say)* it is **moment** *(moh-mah⁽ⁿ⁾)* to learn **les mois** *(mwah)* months **de** *(duh)* of **l'année** *(lah-nay)* the year **et** all the different kinds of **temps.** *(tah⁽ⁿ⁾)* weather

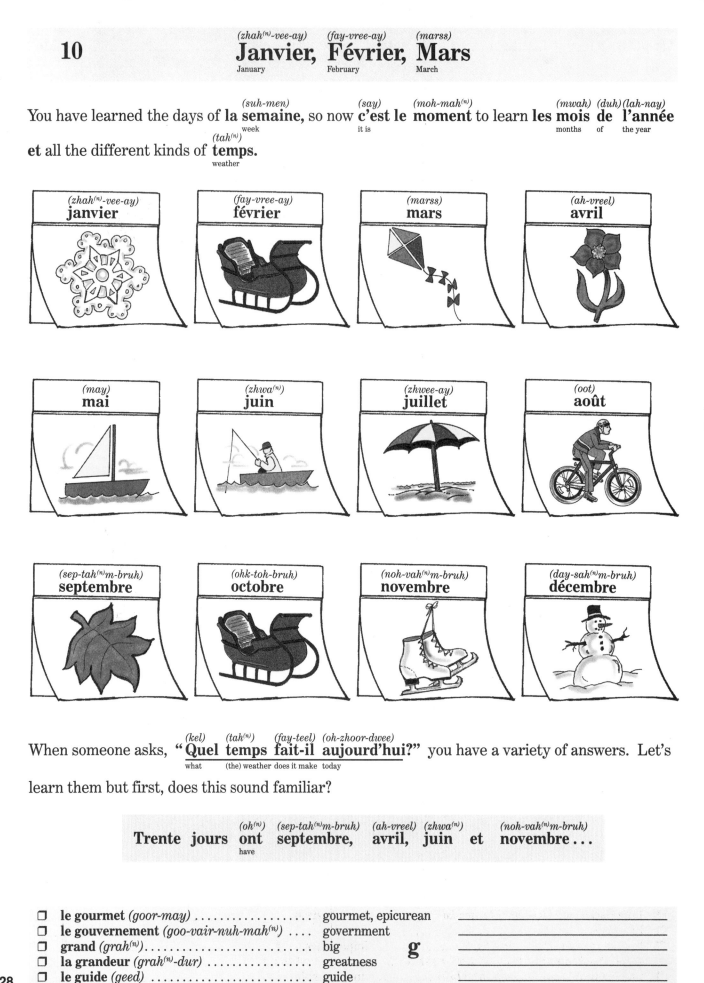

(zhah⁽ⁿ⁾-vee-ay) **janvier**

(fay-vree-ay) **février**

(marss) **mars**

(ah-vreel) **avril**

(may) **mai**

(zhwa⁽ⁿ⁾) **juin**

(zhwee-ay) **juillet**

(oot) **août**

(sep-tah⁽ⁿ⁾m-bruh) **septembre**

(ohk-toh-bruh) **octobre**

(noh-vah⁽ⁿ⁾m-bruh) **novembre**

(day-sah⁽ⁿ⁾m-bruh) **décembre**

When someone asks, "**Quel temps fait-il aujourd'hui?**" you have a variety of answers. Let's
(kel) what   *(tah⁽ⁿ⁾)* (the) weather   *(fay-teel)* does it make   *(oh-zhoor-dwee)* today

learn them but first, does this sound familiar?

Trente jours ont septembre, avril, juin et novembre . . .
(oh⁽ⁿ⁾) have   *(sep-tah⁽ⁿ⁾m-bruh)*   *(ah-vreel)*   *(zhwa⁽ⁿ⁾)*   *(noh-vah⁽ⁿ⁾m-bruh)*

☐ **le gourmet** *(goor-may)* . . . . gourmet, epicurean _____
☐ **le gouvernement** *(goo-vair-nuh-mah⁽ⁿ⁾)* . . . . government _____
☐ **grand** *(grah⁽ⁿ⁾)* . . . . big   **g** _____
☐ **la grandeur** *(grah⁽ⁿ⁾-dur)* . . . . greatness _____
☐ **le guide** *(geed)* . . . . guide _____

(kel) *(tah⁽ⁿ⁾)* *(fay-teel)* *(oh-zhoor-dwee)*
Quel temps fait-il aujourd'hui? _____
what   today

(nehzh) *(ah⁽ⁿ⁾)*
Il neige en janvier. _____
it snows   in

(oh-see)
Il neige aussi en février. _____
      also

(pluh)
Il pleut en mars. _____
it rains

(oh-see)
Il pleut aussi en avril. _____

(fay) *(dew)* *(vah⁽ⁿ⁾)*
Il fait du vent en mai. _____
makes   windy

(soh-lay)
Il fait du soleil en juin. _____
     sunny

(boh)
Il fait beau en juillet. _____
beautiful

(shoh)
Il fait chaud en août. _____
hot

(broo-ee-yar)
Il fait du brouillard en septembre. _____
     foggy

(fay) *(fray)*
Il fait frais en octobre. _____
cool

(moh-vay)
Il fait mauvais en novembre. _____
bad

(fwah)
Il fait froid en décembre. _____
cold

(kel) *(ah⁽ⁿ⁾)*
Quel temps fait-il en février? _____
         in

Quel temps fait-il en avril? _____ Il pleut en avril. Il pleut en avril.

Quel temps fait-il en mai? _____

Quel temps fait-il en août? _____

☐ **l'identification** *(lee-dah⁽ⁿ⁾-tee-fee-kah-syoh⁽ⁿ⁾)* .. identification _____
☐ **l'île** *(leel)* .... island _____
☐ **l'importance** *(la⁽ⁿ⁾-por-tah⁽ⁿ⁾s)* .... importance **i** _____
   – **une chose importante** *(shohz)(a⁽ⁿ⁾-por-tah⁽ⁿ⁾t)*.. an important thing _____
☐ **inacceptable** *(een-ahk-sep-tah-bluh)* .... unacceptable _____

Maintenant, les *(say-zoh(n))* **saisons** de l'année...
seasons   of   the year

(lee-vair)
l'hiver
winter

(lay-tay)
l'été
summer

(loh-tohn)
l'automne
autumn

(prah(n)-tah(n))
le printemps
spring

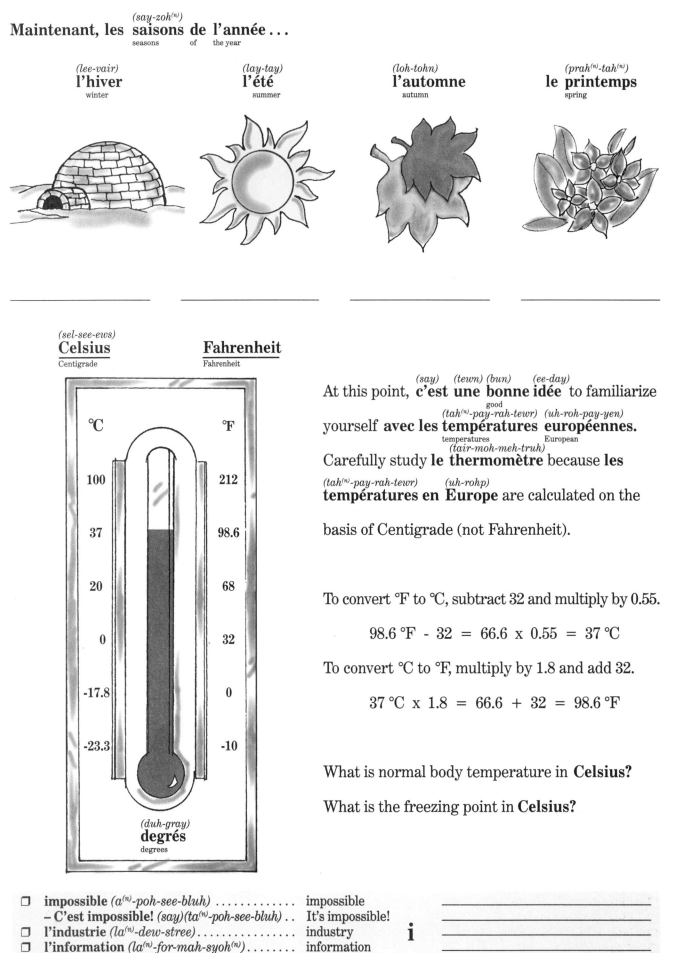

(sel-see-ews)
Celsius
Centigrade

Fahrenheit
Fahrenheit

°C

°F

100 — 212

37 — 98.6

20 — 68

0 — 32

-17.8 — 0

-23.3 — -10

(duh-gray)
degrés
degrees

At this point, *(say) (tewn) (bun) (ee-day)* **c'est une bonne idée** to familiarize
good
yourself **avec les *(tah(n)-pay-rah-tewr)* températures *(uh-roh-pay-yen)* européennes.**
temperatures   European
Carefully study **le thermomètre** *(tair-moh-meh-truh)* because **les**

températures *(tah(n)-pay-rah-tewr)* en Europe *(uh-rohp)* are calculated on the

basis of Centigrade (not Fahrenheit).

To convert °F to °C, subtract 32 and multiply by 0.55.

98.6 °F - 32 = 66.6 x 0.55 = 37 °C

To convert °C to °F, multiply by 1.8 and add 32.

37 °C x 1.8 = 66.6 + 32 = 98.6 °F

What is normal body temperature in **Celsius?**

What is the freezing point in **Celsius?**

☐ **impossible** *(a(n)-poh-see-bluh)* .... impossible
 – **C'est impossible!** *(say)(ta(n)-poh-see-bluh)* .. It's impossible!
☐ **l'industrie** *(la(n)-dew-stree)* .... industry
☐ **l'information** *(la(n)-for-mah-syoh(n))* .... information
☐ **l'ingénieur** *(la(n)-zhay-nyur)* .... engineer

i

(fwah-yay) *(fa⁽ⁿ⁾)* *(fwah)*
Foyer, Faim et Foi!
home   hunger   faith

Just as we have the three "R's" **en anglais, en français** there are the three "F's" which help us

to understand some of the basics of **la vie française et la famille française.** Study the family

(vee) (frah⁽ⁿ⁾-sez)   *(fah-mee-yuh)*

life   French   family

tree below.

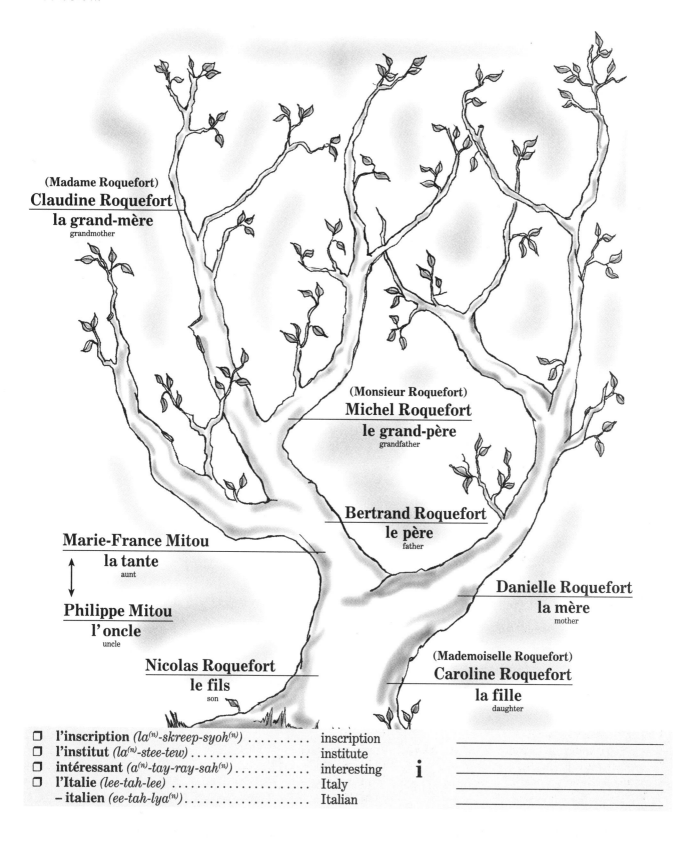

(Madame Roquefort)
Claudine Roquefort
   la grand-mère
      grandmother

(Monsieur Roquefort)
Michel Roquefort
   le grand-père
     grandfather

Bertrand Roquefort
   le père
    father

Marie-France Mitou
   la tante
    aunt

Philippe Mitou
   l'oncle
    uncle

Danielle Roquefort
   la mère
    mother

Nicolas Roquefort
   le fils
    son

(Mademoiselle Roquefort)
Caroline Roquefort
   la fille
    daughter

☐	**l'inscription** *(la⁽ⁿ⁾-skreep-syoh⁽ⁿ⁾)*	inscription	
☐	**l'institut** *(la⁽ⁿ⁾-stee-tew)*	institute	
☐	**intéressant** *(a⁽ⁿ⁾-tay-ray-sah⁽ⁿ⁾)*	interesting	**i**
☐	**l'Italie** *(lee-tah-lee)*	Italy	
	– italien *(ee-tah-lya⁽ⁿ⁾)*	Italian	

Let's learn how to identify **la famille** *(fah-mee-yuh)* family by **nom** *(noh⁽ⁿ⁾)* name. Study the following **exemples** *(eg-zah⁽ⁿ⁾-pluh)* examples carefully.

Comment vous appelez-vous? *(voo) (zah-puh-lay-voo)* _____
what is your name/how are you called

Je m'appelle *(mah-pel)* _____ .
my name is/I am called   (your name)

les parents *(pah-rah⁽ⁿ⁾)*
parents

le père *(pair)* _____
father

Comment s'appelle le père? *(koh-moh⁽ⁿ⁾) (sah-pel)* _____
how   is called   father

la mère *(mair)* _____
mother

Comment s'appelle la mère? _____
how   mother

les enfants *(lay) (zah⁽ⁿ⁾-fah⁽ⁿ⁾)* **Le fils et la fille** *(feess) (fee-yuh)* **sont aussi frère et soeur.** *(frair) (suhr)*
children   brother   sister

le fils *(feess)* _____
son

Comment s'appelle le fils? *(feess)* _____
son

la fille *(fee-yuh)* _____
daughter

Comment s'appelle la fille? *(fee-yuh)* _____
daughter

les parents *(pah-rah⁽ⁿ⁾)*
relatives

le grand-père *(grah⁽ⁿ⁾-pair)* _____
grandfather

Comment s'appelle le grand-père? *(koh-mah⁽ⁿ⁾) (sah-pel)* _____
grandfather

la grand-mère *(grah⁽ⁿ⁾-mair)* _____
grandmother

Comment s'appelle la grand-mère? _____
grandmother

Now you ask —

_____
(How are you called?/What is your name?)

And answer —

_____
(My name is . . .)

❏ **la jaquette** *(zhah-ket)* . . . . woman's jacket _____
❏ **le Japon** *(zhah-poh⁽ⁿ⁾)* . . . . Japan _____
   – **japonais** *(zhah-poh-nay)* . . . . Japanese **j** _____
❏ **le journal** *(zhoor-nahl)* . . . . newspaper _____
❏ **La Joconde** *(zhoh-kohnd)* . . . . Mona Lisa (in the Louvre) _____

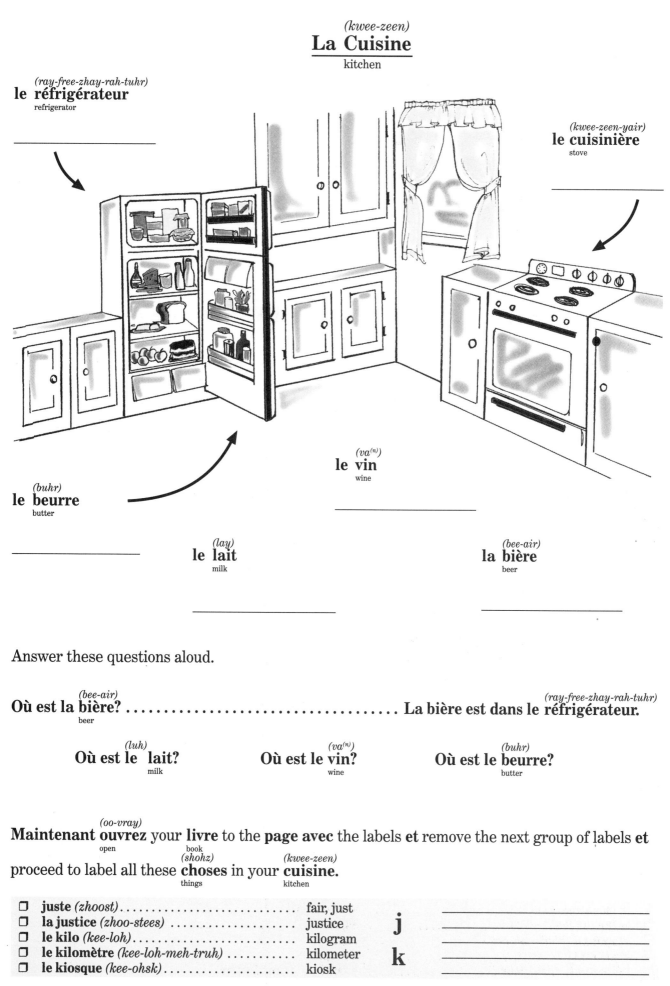

(kwee-zeen)
La Cuisine
kitchen

(ray-free-zhay-rah-tuhr)
le réfrigérateur
refrigerator

_____

(kwee-zeen-yair)
le cuisinière
stove

_____

(buhr)
le beurre
butter

(va⁽ⁿ⁾)
le vin
wine

_____

_____

(lay)
le lait
milk

(bee-air)
la bière
beer

_____

_____

Answer these questions aloud.

(bee-air)
Où est la bière? . . . . *(ray-free-zhay-rah-tuhr)* **La bière est dans le réfrigérateur.**
beer

(luh)
Où est le lait?
milk

(va⁽ⁿ⁾)
Où est le vin?
wine

(buhr)
Où est le beurre?
butter

(oo-vray)
Maintenant ouvrez your **livre** to the **page avec** the labels **et** remove the next group of labels **et**
open   book
(shohz)   *(kwee-zeen)*
proceed to label all these **choses** in your **cuisine.**
things   kitchen

☐	**juste** *(zhoost)*	fair, just	
☐	**la justice** *(zhoo-stees)*	justice	**j** _____
☐	**le kilo** *(kee-loh)*	kilogram	_____
☐	**le kilomètre** *(kee-loh-meh-truh)*	kilometer	**k** _____
☐	**le kiosque** *(kee-ohsk)*	kiosk	_____

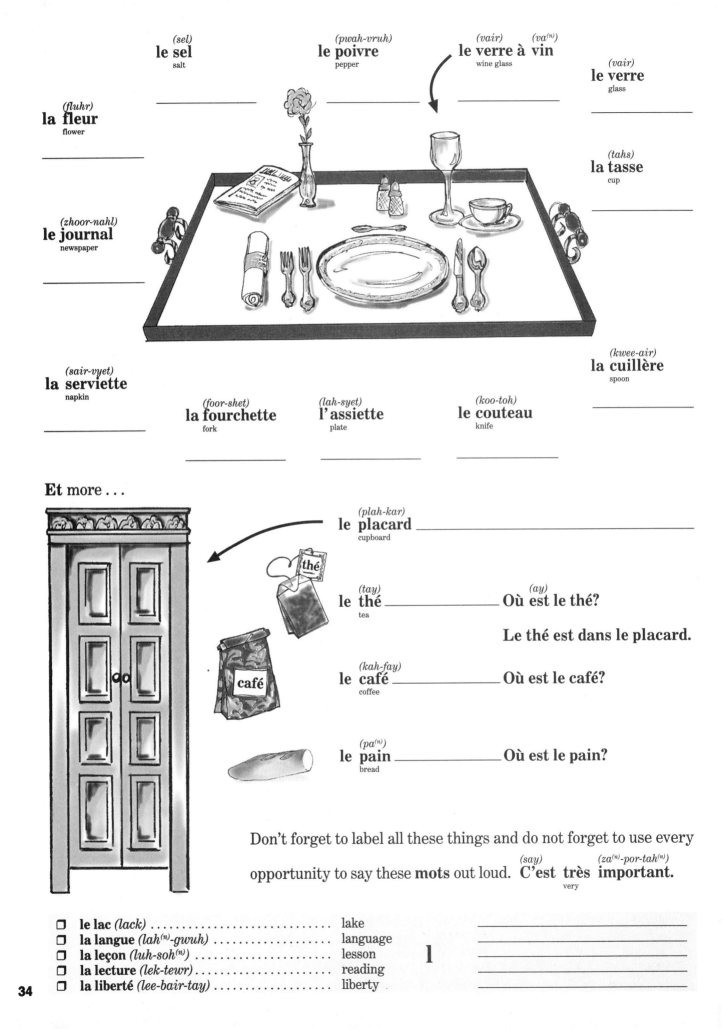

(sel)
le sel
salt

_____

(pwah-vruh)
le poivre
pepper

_____

(vair) *(va⁽ⁿ⁾)*
le verre à vin
wine glass

_____

(vair)
le verre
glass

_____

(fluhr)
la fleur
flower

_____

(tahs)
la tasse
cup

_____

(zhoor-nahl)
le journal
newspaper

_____

(kwee-air)
la cuillère
spoon

_____

(sair-vyet)
la serviette
napkin

_____

(foor-shet)
la fourchette
fork

_____

(lah-syet)
l'assiette
plate

_____

(koo-toh)
le couteau
knife

_____

Et more . . .

(plah-kar)
le placard _____
cupboard

(tay)
le thé _____
tea

(ay)
Où est le thé?

Le thé est dans le placard.

(kah-fay)
le café _____
coffee

Où est le café?

(pa⁽ⁿ⁾)
le pain _____
bread

Où est le pain?

Don't forget to label all these things and do not forget to use every opportunity to say these **mots** out loud. *(say)* **C'est très** *(za⁽ⁿ⁾-por-tah⁽ⁿ⁾)* **important.**
very

☐ **le lac** *(lack)* . . . . lake _____
☐ **la langue** *(lah⁽ⁿ⁾-gwuh)* . . . . language _____
☐ **la leçon** *(luh-soh⁽ⁿ⁾)* . . . . lesson _____
☐ **la lecture** *(lek-tewr)* . . . . reading _____
☐ **la liberté** *(lee-bair-tay)* . . . . liberty _____

l

(par-doh(n))
pardon

(lar-mwahr)
l'armoire

(lee)
le lit

(loh-ray-yay)
l'oreiller

(koo-vair-tewr)
la couverture

(ray-vay)
le réveil

(mir-wahr)
le miroir

(lah-vah-boh)
le lavabo

(sair-vyet)
le serviette

(doo-bul-vay-say)
le W.C.

(doosh)
la douche

(kray-yoh(n))
le crayon

(tay-lay-vee-zur)
la téléviseur

(stee-loh)
le stylo

(lee-vruh)
le livre

(lor-dee-nah-tur)
l'ordinateur

(lew-net)
les lunettes

(pah-pee-ay)
le papier

(kor-bay) *(pah-pee-ay)*
corbeille à papier

(ruh-vew)
la revue

(let-ruh)
la lettre

(ta(n)-bruh-pohst)
le timbre-poste

(kart) *(poh-stahl)*
la carte postale

(pahs-por)
le passeport

(bee-yay)
le billet

(vah-leez)
la valise

(sahk) *(ma(n))*
le sac à main

(port-fuh-yuh)
le portefeuille

(lar-zhah(n))
l'argent

(kart) *(kray-dee)*
les cartes de crédit

(shek) *(vwah-yahzh)*
les chèques de voyage

(lah-pah-ray-foh-toh)
l'appareil-photo

(peh-lee-kewl)
la pellicule

(koh-stewm) *(ba(n))*
le costume de bain

(sah(n)-dahl)
les sandales

(lew-net) *(soh-lay)*
les lunettes de soleil

(brohs) *(dah(n))*
la brosse à dents

(dah(n)-tee-frees)
le dentifrice

(sah-voh(n))
le savon

(rah-zwahr)
le rasoir

(day-oh-doh-rah(n))
le déodorant

(pen-yuh)
le peigne

(mah(n)-toh)
le manteau

(pah-rah-plew-ee)
le parapluie

(la(n)-pair-may-ah-bluh)
l'imperméable

(gah(n))
les gants

(shah-poh)
le chapeau

(boht)
les bottes

(shoh-suhr)
les chaussures

(shoh-suhr) *(teh-nees)*
les chaussures de tennis

(koh(n)-play)
le complet

(krah-vaht)
la cravate

(shuh-meez)
la chemise

(moo-shwahr)
le mouchoir

(veh-stoh(n))
le veston

(pah(n)-tah-loh(n))
le pantalon

(jeans)
les jeans

(short)
le short

(tee-shirt)
le teeshirt

(sleep)
le slip

(tree-koh) *(poh)*
le tricot de peau

(rohb)
la robe

(blooz)
la blouse

(zhewp)
la jupe

(shah(n)-dye)
le chandail

(koh(n)-bee-nay-zoh(n))
la combinaison

(soo-tya(n)-gorzh)
le soutien-gorge

(sleep)
le slip

(shoh-set)
les chaussettes

(bah)
les bas

(pee-zhah-mah)
le pyjama

(shuh-meez) *(nwee)*
la chemise de nuit

(rohb) *(shah(n)-bruh)*
la robe de chambre

(pah(n)-too-fluh)
les pantoufles

(zhuh) *(vya(n))* *(duh)*
Je viens de _____.

(zhuh) *(voo-dray)* *(zah-prah(n)-druh)* *(luh)* *(frah(n)-say)*
Je voudrais apprendre le français.

(zhuh) *(mah-pel)*
Je m'appelle _____.

PLUS...

This book includes a number of other innovative features unique to the *"10 minutes a day®"* series. At the back of this book, you will find twelve pages of flash cards. Cut them out and flip through them at least once a day.

On pages 116, 117 and 118 you will find a beverage guide and a menu guide. Don't wait until your trip to use them. Clip out the menu guide and use it tonight at the dinner table. Take them both with you the next time you dine at your favorite French restaurant.

When you are ready to leave, cut out your Pocket Pal™ and keep it with you at all times! By using the special features in this book, you will be speaking French before you know it.

(ah-mew-zay-voo)   *(bun)*   *(shah$^{(n)}$s)*
Amusez-vous et bonne chance!
enjoy yourself   good   luck

(ruh-lee-zhoh(n))
La Religion
religion

En France, there is not the wide variety of **religions** that **nous avons ici en Amérique.**
(ruh-lee-zhoh(n)) *(noo)* *(zah-voh(n))* *(ee-see)* *(ah-may-reek)*
religions   here

A person is usually one of the following.

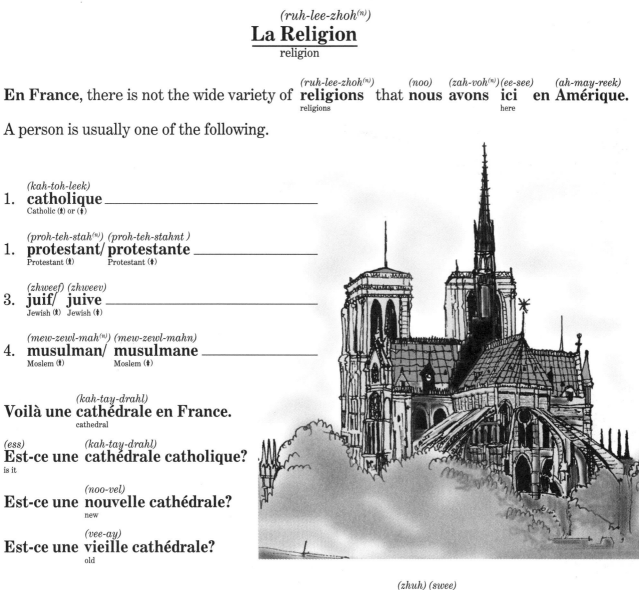

(kah-toh-leek)
1. **catholique** _____
Catholic (♂) or (♀)

(proh-teh-stah(n)) *(proh-teh-stahnt)*
1. **protestant/ protestante** _____
Protestant (♂)   Protestant (♀)

(zhweef) *(zhweev)*
3. **juif/ juive** _____
Jewish (♂)   Jewish (♀)

(mew-zewl-mah(n)) *(mew-zewl-mahn)*
4. **musulman/ musulmane** _____
Moslem (♂)   Moslem (♀)

(kah-tay-drahl)
Voilà une cathédrale en France.
cathedral

(ess) *(kah-tay-drahl)*
Est-ce une cathédrale catholique?
is it

(noo-vel)
Est-ce une nouvelle cathédrale?
new

(vee-ay)
Est-ce une vieille cathédrale?
old

(zhuh) *(swee)*
Maintenant, let's learn how to say "I am" **en français:** **je suis** _____
now   I   am

Test yourself – write each sentence on the next page for more practice. Add your own personal

variations as well.

Note that to make an adjective feminine **en français,** all you *generally* need to do is add an "e."

This will sometimes vary the pronunciation slightly.

(ess) *(kuh)* *(sah)* *(koot)*
_____   _____ **est-ce que ça coûte?**
(how much)   (how much)   does   this   cost

☐	**le lieu** *(lyuh)*	place
☐	**la ligne** *(leen-yuh)*	line
☐	**la limonade** *(lee-moh-nahd)*	lemonade
☐	**le logement** *(lohzh-mah(n))*	lodging, accommodation
☐	**Londres** *(loh(n)-druh)*	London

1

(kah-toh-leek)
Je suis catholique. _____

I   am   Catholic (♀/♂)

(proh-teh-stah⁽ⁿ⁾)
Je suis protestant. _____

(♂)

(swee) *(zhweef)*
Je suis juif. _____

Jewish (♂)

(zhuh) *(ah-may-ree-ka⁽ⁿ⁾)*
Je suis américain. _____

American (♂)

(uh-rohp)
Je suis en Europe. _____

(kah-nah-dyen)
Je suis canadienne. _____

Canadian (♀)

(dah⁽ⁿ⁾) *(lay-gleez)*
Je suis dans l'église. _____

I   am   in   church

(frah⁽ⁿ⁾s)
Je suis en France. _____

(mew-zewl-mah⁽ⁿ⁾)
Je suis musulman. _____

Moslem (♂)

(reh-stoh-rah⁽ⁿ⁾)
Je suis dans le restaurant. _____

(ah-may-ree-ken)
Je suis américaine. _____

(♀)

(loh-tel)
Je suis dans l'hôtel. _____

Je suis dans la maison. _____

I   am

(fah-tee-gay)
Je suis fatigué. _____

I   am   fatigued/tired

(nuh)
To negate any of these statements, simply add "**ne**" before the verb and "**pas**" after the verb.

not/no

(pah)

(nuh)(swee) *(pah)* *(mew-zewl-mah⁽ⁿ⁾)*
Je ne suis pas musulman. _____

I   am not

(pah)
Je ne suis pas français. _____

I   am not

Go through and drill these sentences again but with "**ne**" plus "**pas**."

(fah-mee-yuh)
Maintenant, take a piece of paper. Our **famille** from earlier had a reunion. Identify everyone

(mair) *(loh⁽ⁿ⁾-kluh)*
below by writing **le mot correct en français** for each person — la **mère**, l'**oncle** and so on.

(shya⁽ⁿ⁾)
Don't forget **le chien!**

☐ **le magasin** *(mah-gah-za⁽ⁿ⁾)* . . . . store _____
☐ **le magazine** *(mah-gah-zeen)* . . . . magazine _____
☐ **magnifique** *(mah-nee-feek)* . . . . magnificent   **m** _____
☐ **le marchand** *(mar-shah⁽ⁿ⁾)* . . . . merchant _____
☐ **le mécanicien** *(may-kah-nee-sya⁽ⁿ⁾)* . . . . mechanic _____

(ah-prah⁽ⁿ⁾-druh)

Apprendre!
to learn

You have already used *(duh)* **deux** very important verbs: **je** *(voo-dray)* **voudrais** and **j'ai** *(zhay)*. Although you might
I   would like   I have
be able to get by with only these verbs, let's assume you want to do better. First a quick **review**.

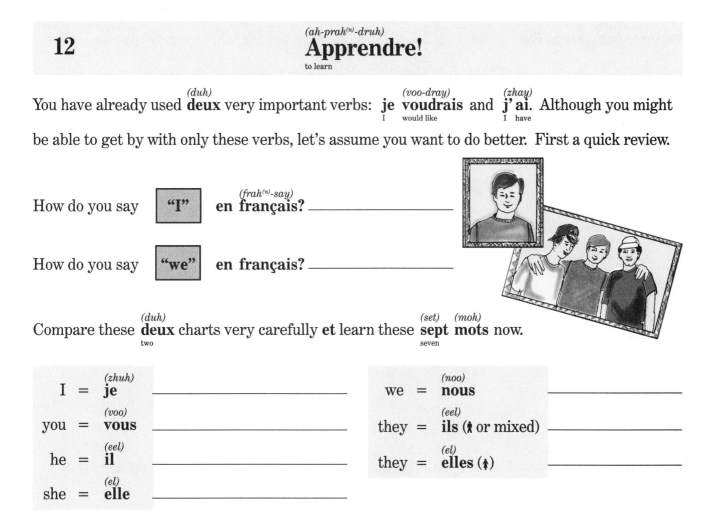

How do you say ⬜ **"I"** *(frah⁽ⁿ⁾-say)* **en français?** _____

How do you say ⬜ **"we"** **en français?** _____

Compare these *(duh)* **deux** charts very carefully **et** learn these **sept** *(set)* **mots** *(moh)* now.
two   seven

I = **je** *(zhuh)* _____	we = **nous** *(noo)* _____
you = **vous** *(voo)* _____	they = **ils** *(eel)* (♂ or mixed) _____
he = **il** *(eel)* _____	they = **elles** *(el)* (♀) _____
she = **elle** *(el)* _____	

Not too hard, is it? Draw lines between the matching **mots** **anglais** *(ah⁽ⁿ⁾-glay)* **et mots** **français** *(frah⁽ⁿ⁾-say)* below to
see if you can keep these **mots** straight in your mind.

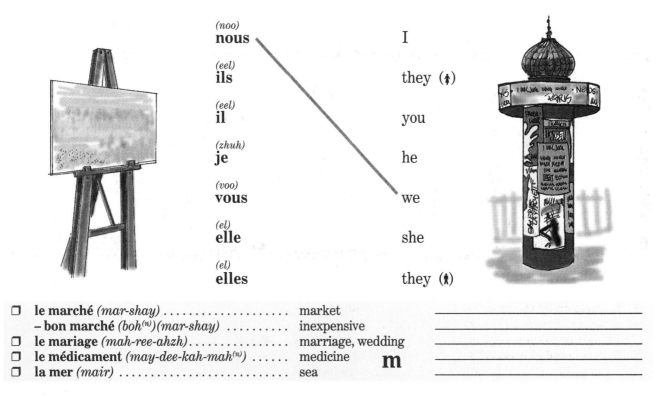

nous *(noo)*   I

ils *(eel)*   they (♂)

il *(eel)*   you

je *(zhuh)*   he

vous *(voo)*   we

elle *(el)*   she

elles *(el)*   they (♀)

☐ **le marché** *(mar-shay)*	market	_____
– **bon marché** *(boh⁽ⁿ⁾)(mar-shay)*	inexpensive	_____
☐ **le mariage** *(mah-ree-ahzh)*	marriage, wedding	_____
☐ **le médicament** *(may-dee-kah-mah⁽ⁿ⁾)*	medicine **m**	_____
☐ **la mer** *(mair)*	sea	_____

Maintenant close **le livre et** write out both columns of this practice on a piece of *(pah-pee-ay)* **papier.** paper How did **vous** do? *(bya⁽ⁿ⁾)* **Bien** well *(mahl)* **ou mal?** or poorly **Maintenant** that **vous** you know these **mots, vous** can say almost anything **en français** with one basic formula: the "plug-in" formula.

To demonstrate, let's take *(seess)* **six** six basic **et** practical verbs **et** see how the "plug-in" formula works. Write the verbs in the blanks after **vous** have practiced saying them out loud many times.

(par-lay) **parler** to speak	_____	*(reh-stay)* **rester** to remain, to stay	_____
(ah-bee-tay) **habiter** to live, to reside	*habiter, habiter*	*(koh-mah⁽ⁿ⁾-day)* **commander** to order	_____
(ah-shuh-tay) **acheter** to buy	_____	*(sah-puh-lay)* **s'appeler** to be called	_____

Besides the familiar words already circled, can **vous** find the above verbs in the puzzle below?

When **vous** find them, write them in the blanks to the right.

P	C	O	M	M	A	N	D	E	R	H
A	O	C	N	P	C	Q	U	I	E	A
R	M	D	O	Y	H	V	J	J	S	B
L	M	R	S	O	E	E	B	O	T	I
E	E	M	E	Ù	T	L	U	Y	E	T
R	N	D	I	R	E	T	M	N	R	E
V	T	N	I	L	R	B	D	E	I	R
S	'	A	P	P	E	L	E	R	H	T

1. _____

2. _____

3. _____

4. _____

5. _____

6. _____

☐ **le métro** *(may-troh)* . . . . subway, metro
☐ **la minute** *(mee-newt)* . . . . minute
  – **la minuterie** *(mee-new-tuh-ree)* . . . . automatic light switch
☐ **la mode** *(mohd)* . . . . fashion
  – **à la mode** *(ah)(lah)(mohd)* . . . . fashionable

m

_____
_____
_____
_____

40

Study the following patterns carefully.

je *(zhuh)* **il** *(eel)* **elle** *(el)*	*(parl)* **parle**	=	I *speak* he/she *speaks*
	(ah-beet) **habite**	=	I *live* he/she *lives*
	(ah-shet) **achète**	=	I *buy* he/she *buys*
	(rest) **reste**	=	I *remain* he/she *remains*
	(koh-mah(n)d) **commande**	=	I *order* he/she *orders*
je	*(mah-pel)* **m'appelle**	=	I *am called*
il/elle	*(sah-pel)* **s'appelle**	=	he/she *is called*

nous *(noo)*	*(par-loh(n))* **parlons**	=	we *speak*
	(zah-bee-toh(n)) **habitons**	=	we *live*
	(zah-shuh-toh(n)) **achetons**	=	we *buy*
	(reh-stoh(n)) **restons**	=	we *remain*
	(koh-mah(n)-doh(n)) **commandons**	=	we *order*
nous *(noo)*	**nous appelons** *(noo)* *(zah-puh-loh(n))*	=	we *are called/* *our name is*

Note: • With all these verbs, the first thing you do is drop the final "**er**," "**ir**," or "**re**" from the basic verb form or stem.

• With "**je**," "**il**," or "**elle**," add "**e**" to the basic verb form.

• With "**nous**," add "**ons**."

• **S'appeler** varies but not too much. It is a very important verb so take a few extra minutes to learn it.

Some verbs just will not conform to the pattern! But don't worry. Speak slowly **et** clearly, **et** you will be perfectly understood whether you say "**parle**" or "**parlons**." French speakers will be delighted that you have taken the time to learn their language.

Note: • French has two separate and very different ways of saying "you" whereas in English we only use one word.

• "**Vous**" *(voo)* will be used throughout this book and will be appropriate for most situations. "**Vous**" refers to one person in a formal sense as well as being the plural in both a formal and informal sense. _{you}

• "**Tu**" *(too)* is a form of address reserved for family members and very close friends. _{you (singular)}

❏	**le monde** *(mohnd)*	world	
	– **tout le monde** *(too)(luh)(mohnd)*	everyone	
❏	**la montagne** *(moh(n)-tahn-yuh)*	mountain	**m**
❏	**le musée** *(mew-zay)*	museum	
❏	**la musique** *(mew-zeek)*	music	

Here's your next group of patterns!

	(par-lay) **parlez**	= you *speak*
	(zah-bee-tay) **habitez**	= you *live*
(voo) **vous**	*(zah-shuh-tay)* **achetez**	= you *buy*
	(reh-stay) **restez**	= you *remain*
	(koh-mah⁽ⁿ⁾-day) **commandez**	= you *order*
(voo) **vous**	*(voo)* **vous** *(zah-puh-lay)* **appelez**	= you *are called* your name is

	(parl) **parlent**	= they *speak*
	(zah-beet) **habitent**	= they *live*
(eel) **ils** *(el)* **elles**	*(zah-shet)* **achètent**	= they *buy*
	(rest) **restent**	= they *remain*
	(koh-mah⁽ⁿ⁾d) **commandent**	= they *order*
ils/elles	*(sah-pel)* **s'appellent**	= they *are called* their name is

Note: • Notice that despite differences in spelling, many of the verbs are pronounced the same.

• With "**vous**," add "**ez**" to the basic verb form.

• With "**ils**," and "**elles**" simply add "**ent**" to the basic verb form. The "**ent**" is silent.

(vwah-lah)(seess)
Voilà six more verbs.
here are   six

(vuh-neer)
venir _____
to come

(ah-prah⁽ⁿ⁾-druh)
apprendre _____
to learn

(voo-dray)
voudrais _____
(I) would like

(ah-lay)
aller _____
to go

(ah-vwahr)
avoir _____ *avoir, avoir*
to have

(ah-vwahr) (buh-zwa⁽ⁿ⁾) (duh)
avoir besoin de _____
to need, to have need of

At the back of **le livre, vous** will find twelve

(pahzh)
pages of flash cards to help you learn these
pages
(noo-voh)
nouveaux mots. Cut them out; carry them in
new

(oo)
your briefcase, purse, pocket **ou** knapsack; **et**
or

review them whenever **vous** have a free moment.

❏	**la nation** *(nah-syoh⁽ⁿ⁾)*	nation	
❏	**la nature** *(nah-tewr)*	nature	
❏	**naturel** *(nah-tew-rel)*.....................	natural	**n**
	– au naturel *(oh)(nah-tew-rel)*............	plain, simple	
❏	**la nécessité** *(nay-seh-see-tay)*	necessity	

Maintenant, it is your turn to practice what **vous** *(voo)* have learned. Fill in the following blanks with the correct form of the verb. Each time **vous** write out the sentence, be sure to say it aloud.

(par-lay)
parler
to speak

Je _____ français. *(frah⁽ⁿ⁾-say)*

Vous _____ anglais. *(ah⁽ⁿ⁾-glay)*

Il _____ espagnol. *(eh-spahn-yohl)*
Elle Spanish

Nous _____ japonais. *(zhah-poh-nay)*
Japanese

Ils _____ allemand. *(ahl-mah⁽ⁿ⁾)*
Elles German

(ah-bee-tay)
habiter
to live, to reside

J' *habite/* _____ en France. *(frah⁽ⁿ⁾s)*

Vous _____ en Italie. *(ee-tah-lee)*

Il _____ en Europe. *(uh-rohp)*
Elle

Nous _____ en Chine. *(sheen)*

Ils _____ en Japon. *(zhah-poh⁽ⁿ⁾)*
Elles

(ah-shuh-tay)
acheter
to buy

J' *achète/* _____ un livre. *(lee-vruh)*

Vous _____ une salade. *(sah-lahd)*

Il _____ une horloge. *(or-lohzh)*
Elle clock

Nous _____ trois tickets d'autobus. *(tee-kay)* *(doh-toh-boos)*

Ils _____ sept timbres-post. *(ta⁽ⁿ⁾-bruh-pohst)*
Elles

(reh-stay)
rester
to remain, to stay

Je _____ en France. *(frah⁽ⁿ⁾s)*

Vous *restez/* _____ en Amérique.

Il _____ en Belgique. *(bel-zheek)*
Elle Belgium

Nous _____ en Allemagne. *(ahl-mahn-yuh)*
Germany

Ils _____ en Espagne. *(eh-spahn-yuh)*
Elles Spain

(koh-mah⁽ⁿ⁾-day)
commander
to order

Je _____ un verre de vin. *(vair)* *(va⁽ⁿ⁾)*

Vous _____ une tasse de thé. *(tahs)*

Il _____ une tasse de café.
Elle

Nous _____ deux verres d'eau. *(duh)* *(vair)* *(doh)*
water

Ils _____ trois verres de lait. *(twah)* *(lay)*
Elles milk

(sah-puh-lay)
s'appeler
to be called

Je _____ Jeanne.

Vous _____ Mitou.

Il _____ Smith.
Elle

Nous _____ Roquefort.

Ils _____ Vartan.
Elles

❑ **neuf** *(nuf)*	new	_____
– **Le Pont Neuf à Paris** *(poh⁽ⁿ⁾)(nuf)*	new bridge in Paris (1604)	
❑ **Noël** *(noh-el)*	Christmas **n**	_____
❑ **le nord** *(nor)*	north	_____
❑ **Notre-Dame de Paris** *(noh-truh)(dahm)*	Our Lady of Paris (cathedral)	_____

Now take a break, walk around the room, take a deep breath **et** do the next **six** *(seess)* verbs.

(vuh-neer)
venir
to come

Je <u>viens/</u> d'Amérique.

Vous <u>venez/</u> de Belgique.

Il <u>vient/</u> du Canada.
Elle

Nous <u>venons/</u> de New York.

Ils <u>viennent/</u> de Suisse. *(swees)*
Elles   Switzerland

(ah-lay)
aller
to go

Je <u>vais/</u> en France.

Vous <u>allez/</u> en Italie. *(ee-tah-lee)*

Il <u>va/</u> en Angleterre.
Elle

Nous <u>allons/</u> en Belgique. *(bel-zheek)*

Ils <u>vont/</u> en Europe. *(uh-rohp)*
Elles

(ah-prah$^{(n)}$-druh)
apprendre
to learn

J'<u>apprends/</u> l'anglais.

Vous <u>apprenez/</u> le français.

Il <u>apprend/</u> l'italien.
Elle

Nous <u>apprenons/</u> l'allemand.

Ils <u>apprennent/</u> l'espagnol.
Elles   Spanish

(ah-vwahr)
avoir
to have

J'<u>ai/</u> dix francs. *(deess)(frah$^{(n)}$)*

Vous <u>avez/</u> cent francs.

Il <u>a/</u> vingt francs. *(va$^{(n)}$)*
Elle

Nous <u>avons/</u> cinquante francs. *(sang-kah$^{(n)}$t)*

Ils <u>ont/</u> cinq cents francs. *(sank)(sah$^{(n)}$)*
Elles

(voo-dray)
voudrais
(I) would like

Je <u>voudrais/</u> un verre de vin. *(vair)(va$^{(n)}$)*

Vous <u>voudriez/</u> un verre de vin rouge. *(roozh)*

Il <u>voudrait/</u> deux verres de vin blanc.
Elle

Nous <u>voudrions/</u> trois verres de vin. *(vair)*

Ils <u>voudraient/</u> deux verres de lait. *(lay)*
Elles

(ah-vwahr)(buh-zwa$^{(n)}$)(duh)
avoir besoin de
to have need of, to need

J'<u>ai besoin/</u> d'un verre d'eau. *(duh$^{(n)}$)(doh)*

Vous _____ d'une tasse de thé. *(dewn)*

Il _____ de deux tasses de thé.
Elle

Nous _____ de trois tasses de café.

Ils _____ de cinq verres de bière.
Elles

☐ **l'objet** *(lohb-zhay)* . . . . object   _____
☐ **obligatoire** *(oh-blee-gah-twahr)* . . . . compulsory, obligatory   _____
☐ **l'observation** *(lohb-sair-vah-syoh$^{(n)}$)* . . . . . . observation   **O**   _____
☐ **l'occupation** *(loh-kew-pah-syoh$^{(n)}$)* . . . . profession, occupation   _____
☐ **l'odeur** *(loh-dur)* . . . . smell, odor

44

Oui, *(wee)* it is hard to get used to all those **nouveaux** *(noo-voh)* **mots.** *(moh)* Just keep practicing **et** before **vous** *(voo)*
yes

know it, **vous** will be using them naturally. **Maintenant** is a perfect time to turn to the back of

this **livre,** clip out your verb flash cards **et** start flashing. Don't skip over your free **mots** either.

Check them off in the box provided as **vous apprenez** *(ah-preh-nay)* each one. See if **vous** can fill in the
learn

blanks below. **Les réponses correctes sont** at the bottom of **la page.**

1. _____
(I speak French.)

2. _____
(We learn French.)

3. _____
(She needs ten francs.)

4. _____
(He comes from Canada.)

5. _____
(They live in France.)

6. _____
(You buy a book.)

In the following Steps, **vous** will be intro-

duced to more verbs **et vous** should drill them

in exactly the same way as **vous** did in this

section. Look up **les nouveaux mots** in your

(deek-syoh-nair)
dictionnaire et make up your own sentences.
dictionary

Try out your **nouveaux mots** for that's how

you make them yours to use on your holiday.

Remember, the more **vous** practice

maintenant, the more enjoyable your trip

will be. **Bonne** *(bun)* **chance!** *(shah⁽ⁿ⁾s)*
good luck

45

13   *(kel)* *(uhr)* *(ay-teel)* **Quelle heure est-il?**
what time is it

Vous know how to tell **les** *(zhoor)* **jours de la** *(suh-men)* **semaine et les** *(mwah)* **mois de l'** *(lah-nay)* **année,** so now let's learn to tell
days   week   months   year

time. As a *(vwah-yah-zhur)* **voyageur, vous** need to be able to tell time in order to make **réservations,**
traveler

(rah⁽ⁿ⁾-day-voo) **rendez-vous et** to catch **trains et autobus. Voilà les** "basics."
appointments   here are

What time is it?	=	*(kel)* *(uhr)* *(ay-teel)* **Quelle heure est-il?** _____
hour	=	*(uhr)* **heure** _____
noon	=	*(mee-dee)* **midi** _____
midnight	=	*(mee-nwee)* **minuit** _____
half past	=	*(duh-mee)* **et demie** _____
minus/less	=	*(mwa⁽ⁿ⁾)* **moins** _____
a quarter	=	*(kar)* **un quart** _____
a quarter to	=	*(mwa⁽ⁿ⁾)* *(kar)* **moins le quart** _____
a quarter after	=	*(kar)* **et quart** _____

Maintenant quiz yourself. Fill in the missing letters below.

midnight = m _ n u _ t   less = m o _ _ s

a quarter to = m o i _ s ✕ l e ✕ q _ _ r t

half past = e _ ✕ d _ m _ e   hour = h _ _ r e

and finally   when = _ _ _ n d

☐ **occupé** *(oh-kew-pay)* . . . . busy, occupied   _____
   – une ligne occupée . . . . engaged telephone line   _____
☐ **officiel** *(oh-fee-syel)* . . . . official   _____
☐ **l'orchestre** *(lor-kess-truh)* . . . . orchestra   **o**   _____
☐ **l'Orient** *(loh-ree-ah⁽ⁿ⁾)* . . . . Orient   _____

Maintenant, **comment** *(koh-mah(n))* (how) are these **mots** used? Study **les exemples** *(eg-zah(n)-pluh)* (examples) below. When **vous** think it through, it really is not too difficult. Just notice that the pattern changes after the halfway mark.

Notice that the phrase "o'clock" is not used in French.

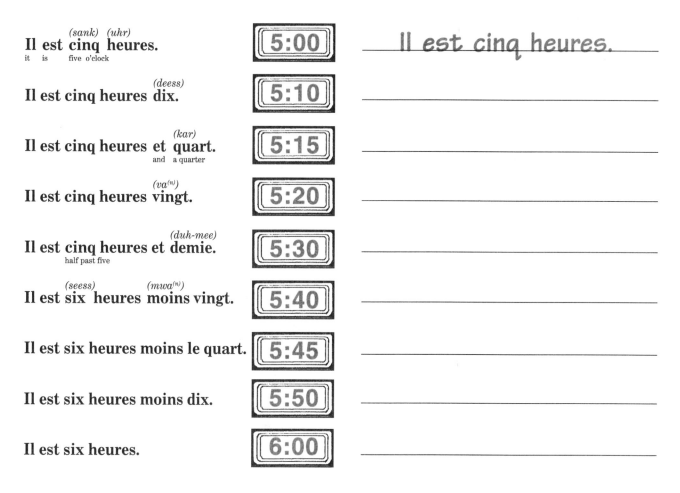

Il est cinq heures. *(sank) (uhr)*
it is five o'clock — 5:00 — *Il est cinq heures.*

Il est cinq heures dix. *(deess)* — 5:10

Il est cinq heures et quart. *(kar)*
and a quarter — 5:15

Il est cinq heures vingt. *(va(n))* — 5:20

Il est cinq heures et demie. *(duh-mee)*
half past five — 5:30

Il est six heures moins vingt. *(seess) (mwa(n))* — 5:40

Il est six heures moins le quart. — 5:45

Il est six heures moins dix. — 5:50

Il est six heures. — 6:00

See how **important** it is to learn **les nombres**? *(nohm-bruh)* Answer the **questions** *(kes-tyoh(n))* (questions) **suivantes** *(swee-vah(n)t)* (following) based on **les horloges** *(or-lohzh)* (clocks) below. **Quelle** *(kel)* **heure est-il?** *(ay-teel)*

1. 8:00 _____

2. 7:15 _____

3. 4:30 _____

4. 9:20 _____

When **vous** answer a "**Quand?**" *(kah(n))* *when* question, say "**à**" *(ah)* *at* before **vous** give the time.

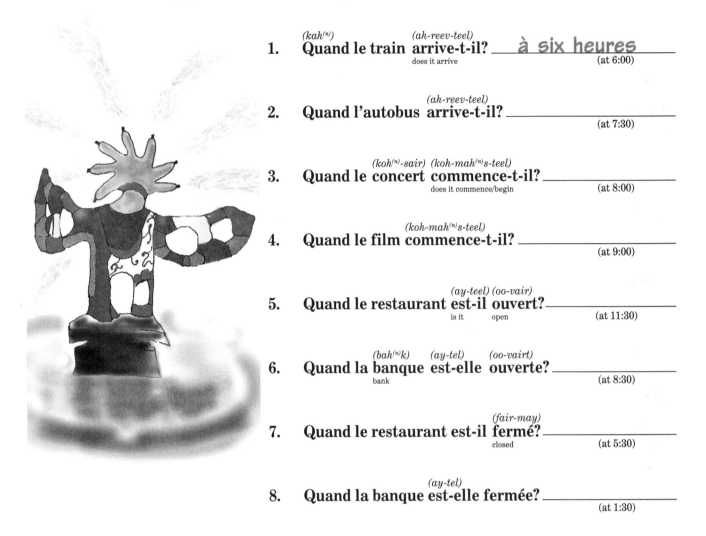

1. **Quand le train arrive-t-il?** *(kah(n))* *(ah-reev-teel)* *does it arrive* _à six heures_ (at 6:00)

2. **Quand l'autobus arrive-t-il?** *(ah-reev-teel)* _____ (at 7:30)

3. **Quand le concert commence-t-il?** *(koh(n)-sair)* *(koh-mah(n)s-teel)* *does it commence/begin* _____ (at 8:00)

4. **Quand le film commence-t-il?** *(koh-mah(n)s-teel)* _____ (at 9:00)

5. **Quand le restaurant est-il ouvert?** *(ay-teel)* *(oo-vair)* *is it* *open* _____ (at 11:30)

6. **Quand la banque est-elle ouverte?** *(bah(n)k)* *(ay-tel)* *(oo-vairt)* *bank* _____ (at 8:30)

7. **Quand le restaurant est-il fermé?** *(fair-may)* *closed* _____ (at 5:30)

8. **Quand la banque est-elle fermée?** *(ay-tel)* _____ (at 1:30)

Voilà a quick quiz. Fill in the blanks **avec** *(ah-vek)* *with* **les nombres corrects.**

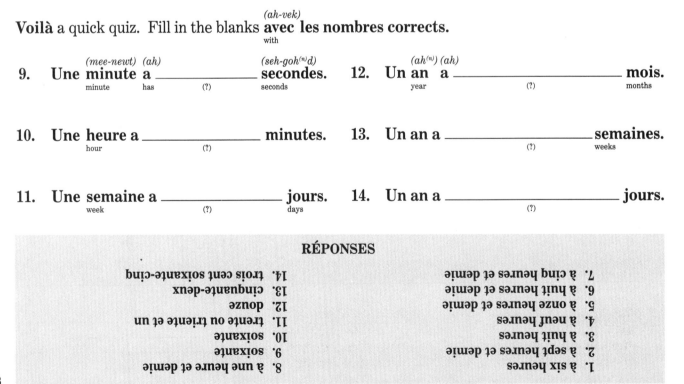

9. **Une minute a** *(mee-newt)* *(ah)* *minute* *has* _____ **secondes.** *(seh-goh(n)d)* *seconds* (?)

10. **Une heure a** *hour* _____ **minutes.** (?)

11. **Une semaine a** *week* _____ **jours.** *days* (?)

12. **Un an a** *(ah(n))* *(ah)* *year* _____ **mois.** *months* (?)

13. **Un an a** _____ **semaines.** *weeks* (?)

14. **Un an a** _____ **jours.** (?)

Do **vous** remember your greetings from earlier? It is a good time to review them as they will

always be **très** **importantes.** *(za⁽ⁿ⁾-por-tah⁽ⁿ⁾-tuh)*
very   important

(wheat) (uhr)   (dew)   (oh⁽ⁿ⁾) (dee)   (mah-dahm) (dew-poh⁽ⁿ⁾)
À huit heures du matin on dit, "Bonjour, Madame Dupont."
at   morning   says good morning Mrs.

(kess)   (koh⁽ⁿ⁾) (dee)
Qu'est-ce qu'on dit? _____ Bonjour, Madame Dupont. _____
what   does one say

(ewn)
À une heure de l'après-midi on dit, "Bonjour, Monsieur Monet." *(muh-syur)*
one   afternoon   Mr.

(kess)   (koh⁽ⁿ⁾) (dee)
Qu'est-ce qu'on dit? _____

À huit heures du soir on dit, "Bonsoir, Mademoiselle Vartan." *(mahd-mwah-zel)*
                                              Miss

Qu'est-ce qu'on dit? _____

(deess)   (swahr)   (bun)   (nwee) (muh-syur)
À dix heures du soir on dit, "Bonne nuit, Monsieur Mitou."
ten   good   night

Qu'est-ce qu'on dit? _____

Vous have probably already noticed that plurals are *generally* formed by adding "s".

(vwah-tewr)	*(lay) (vwah-tewr)*
la voiture	**les voitures**
the car	the cars
(lee-vruh)	
le livre	**les livres**
book	books
(kart)	
la carte	**les cartes**
map	maps

Where to place the accent in French need never be a problem. **Les mots français** *(lay) (frah⁽ⁿ⁾-say)* are always

accented on the last syllable. It's easy. Don't be afraid of all the extra hyphens, apostrophes,

accents and uncommon squiggles in French. Concentrate on your easy pronunciation guide and

remember – practice, practice, practice.

(ess)	*(kess) (kuh) (say)*	*(sah-pel)*	*(kess) (koh⁽ⁿ⁾)*
est-ce	**qu'est-ce que c'est**	**il s'appelle**	**qu'est-ce qu'on**
is it	what is that	he is called	what does one

❑ **l'omelette** *(lohm-let)* .... omelette _____
❑ **on** *(oh⁽ⁿ⁾)* .... one, people, they, we _____
– **On fait ça.** *(oh⁽ⁿ⁾)(fay)(sah)* .... One does that. **O** _____
– **On dit que ...** *(oh⁽ⁿ⁾)(dee)(kuh)* .... One says that ... _____
❑ **l'optimiste** *(lohp-tee-meest)* .... optimist _____

Voilà deux new verbs *(poor)* **pour** (for) Step 13.

(mah$^{(n)}$-zhay) **manger** (to eat) ______________________

(bwahr) **boire** (to drink) ______________________

(mah$^{(n)}$-zhay)
manger
to eat

Je	mange/	une *(sah-lahd)* salade.
Vous	______________	de la *(soup)* soupe (soup).
Il / Elle	______________	*(boh-koo)* beaucoup (very much).
Nous	mangeons/	des *(ess-kar-goh)* escargots (snails).
Ils ne / Elles	mangent/	*(rya$^{(n)}$)* rien.

(bwahr)
boire
to drink

Je	bois/	du *(lay)* lait.
Vous ne	buvez/	*(rya$^{(n)}$)* rien (nothing).
Il / Elle	boit/	du vin blanc.
Nous	buvons/	des bières.
Ils / Elles	boivent/	du thé.

Remember, to negate a statement, add "*(nuh)* **ne**" before the verb and "*(pah)* **pas**" after the verb. Notice in the examples above, that when you used the word "*(rya$^{(n)}$)* **rien** (nothing)," you also added "**ne**" before the verb.

Je *(nuh)* **ne** *(mah$^{(n)}$zh)* **mange** (eat) **rien** (nothing).

Nous (we) **ne commandons** (order) **rien** (nothing).

Je *(nuh)* **ne** (do not) **parle** (speak) *(pah)* **pas français.**

Nous ne venons (do not come) **pas du Canada.**

O

- ❒ **ordinaire** *(or-dee-nair)* . . . . ordinary ______________
- ❒ **organisé** *(or-gah-nee-zay)* . . . . organized ______________
- ❒ **l'origine** *(loh-ree-zheen)* . . . . origin ______________
  - **– Je suis d'origine américaine.** . . . . I come from the USA originally. ______________
- ❒ **l'ouest** *(luh-west)* . . . . west ______________

Vous have learned a lot of material in the last few steps **et** that means it is time to quiz yourself. Don't panic, this is just for you **et** no one else needs to know how **vous** did. Remember, this is a chance to review, find out what **vous** remember **et** what **vous** need to spend more time on. After **vous** have finished, check your **réponses** in the glossary at the back of this book. Circle the correct answers.

le café	tea	coffee
oui	yes	no
la tante	aunt	uncle
ou	and	or
apprendre	to drink	to learn
la nuit	morning	night
vendredi	Friday	Tuesday
parler	to live	to speak
l'hiver	summer	winter
l'argent	money	page
dix	nine	ten
beaucoup	a lot	bread

la famille	seven	family
les enfants	children	grandfather
le lait	butter	(milk)
le sel	pepper	salt
sous	under	over
l'homme	man	doctor
juin	June	July
la cuisine	kitchen	religions
j'ai	I would like	I have
acheter	to order	to buy
hier	yesterday	tomorrow
bon	good	yellow

(koh-mah⁽ⁿ⁾) *(tah-lay-voo)*
Comment allez-vous?   What time is it?   How are you?   Well, how are you after this quiz?

- ☐ **la paire** *(pair)* . . . . pair   _____
- ☐ **le pantalon** *(pah⁽ⁿ⁾-tah-loh⁽ⁿ⁾)* . . . . pair of trousers   _____
- ☐ **le Pape** *(pahp)* . . . . Pope   _____
- ☐ **parfait** *(par-fay)* . . . . perfect   **p**   _____
- – **C'est parfait.** *(say)(par-fay)* . . . . That's fine.   _____

51

(nor) *(sood)* *(est)* *(west)*

Nord - Sud, Est - Ouest

north   south   east   west

If **vous** are looking at **une** *(kart)* **carte et vous** see **les mots** *(swee-vah⁽ⁿ⁾)* **suivants**, it should not be too difficult to

map

figure out what they mean. Take an educated guess.

(lah-may-reek) (dew) (nor)
l'Amérique du nord

(pohl)
le Pôle nord

(dew) (sood)
l'Amérique du sud

(pohl)
le Pôle sud

(koht) (duh) (lest)
la côte de l'est

(lah-freek)
l'Afrique du sud

(luh-west)
la côte de l'ouest

(leer-lahnd) (nor)
l'Irelande du nord

Les mots français pour "north," "south," "east," **et** "west" are easy to recognize due to their

similarity to **anglais.** These **mots** *(treh) (za⁽ⁿ⁾-por-tah⁽ⁿ⁾)* **sont très importants.** Learn them **aujourd'hui!**

are

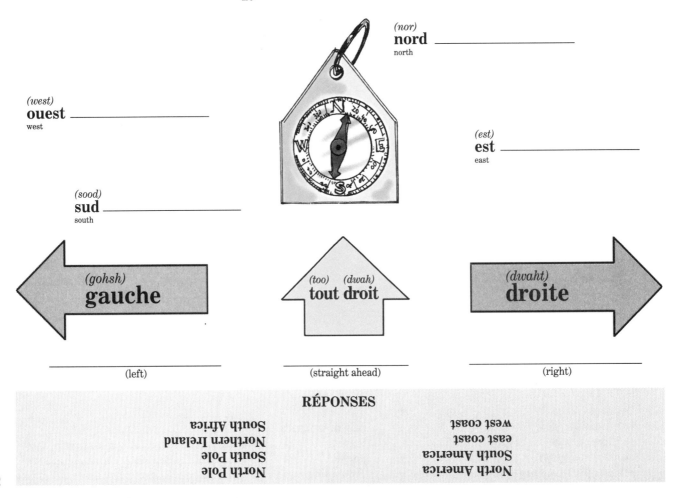

(nor)
nord _____
north

(west)
ouest _____
west

(est)
est _____
east

(sood)
sud _____
south

(gohsh)
gauche

(too) (dwah)
tout droit

(dwaht)
droite

_____ (left)   _____ (straight ahead)   _____ (right)

These **mots** can go a long way. Say them aloud each time you write them in the blanks below.

(seel) (voo) (play)
s'il vous plaît _____
please

(mair-see)
merci _____
thank you

(par-doh⁽ⁿ⁾) (ek-skew-zay-mwah)
pardon/excusez-moi _____
excuse me

(duh)(rya⁽ⁿ⁾)
de rien _____
you're welcome

Voilà deux *(koh⁽ⁿ⁾-vair-sah-syoh⁽ⁿ⁾)* **conversations très** *(tee-peek)* **typiques pour** someone who is trying to find something. Write
two   conversations   very   typical   for

them out in the blanks below.

Jean Paul: **Excusez-moi,** *(may)* **mais où est l'Hôtel** *(loh-tel)* **Cézanne?**
but

<u>   **Excusez-moi, mais où est l'Hôtel Cézanne?** </u>

Claude: *(koh⁽ⁿ⁾-tee-new-ay)* **Continuez tout droit.** *(toor-nay)* **Tournez à gauche à la** *(duh-zee-em)* **deuxième** *(rew)* **rue.**
continue   turn   to the left   second   street

_____

L'Hôtel Cézanne est à droite.
on the right

_____

Thomas: **Pardon, Monsieur. Où est le** *(moo-zay)* **Musée** *(dor-say)* **d'Orsay?**
museum

_____

Christine: *(toor-nay)* **Tournez à droite** *(ee-see)* **ici. Continuez** *(ah⁽ⁿ⁾-vee-roh⁽ⁿ⁾)* **environ** *(sah⁽ⁿ⁾)* **cent** *(meh-truh)* **mètres.**
turn   here   about   meters

_____

Le Musée d'Orsay est à gauche.
on the left

❏ **le parc** *(park)*	park	_____
❏ **le parfum** *(par-fuh⁽ⁿ⁾)*	perfume	_____
– **la parfumerie** *(par-few-muh-ree)*	perfume shop **p**	_____
❏ **le parking** *(par-keeng)*	parking lot	_____
❏ **le passeport** *(pahs-por)*	passport	_____

Are **vous** lost? There is no need to be lost if **vous avez** *(voo)* *(zah-vay)* learned the basic **mots de direction.** *(dee-rek-syoh⁽ⁿ⁾)*
have

Do not try to memorize these **conversations** because **vous** will never be looking for precisely

these places. One day, **vous** might need to ask for **directions** to "**le Louvre**" *(loo-vruh)* or "**l'Hôtel**

Maurice." Learn the key direction **mots et** be sure **vous** can find your destination. **Vous** may

want to buy a guidebook to start planning which places **vous** would like to visit. Practice asking

directions to these special places. What if the person responding to *your* **question** answers too

quickly for **vous** to understand the entire reply? Practice saying,

Excusez-moi. Je *(zhuh)* **ne** *(nuh)* **comprends** *(koh⁽ⁿ⁾-prah⁽ⁿ⁾)* **pas.** *(pah)* **Répétez,** *(ray-pay-tay)* **s'il vous plaît. Merci.**
do not understand   repeat

Maintenant, say it again **et** then write it out below.

_____

(Excuse me. I do not understand. Please repeat. Thank you.)

Oui, c'est difficile *(wee)* *(dee-fee-seel)* at first but don't give up! **Quand** the directions are repeated, **vous** will be able
yes   difficult   when

to understand if **vous avez** *(voo)* *(zah-vay)* learned the key **mots.** Let's review by writing them in the blanks below.

right

left

_____
(north)

_____
(west)

_____
(east)

_____
(south)

❑	**la pâtisserie** *(pah-tee-suh-ree)*	pastry, pastry shop	_____
❑	**le peuple français** *(puh-pluh)(frah⁽ⁿ⁾-say)* ...	French people	_____
❑	**la pharmacie** *(far-mah-see)*...............	pharmacy **p**	_____
❑	**la photo** *(foh-toh)*.....................	photo	_____
❑	**la pilule** *(pee-lewl)*.....................	pill	_____

(vwah-lah) (kah-truh) (noo-voh)
Voilà quatre nouveaux verbes.
new

(deer)
dire _____
to say

(koh(n)-prah(n)-druh)
comprendre _____
to understand

(vah(n)-druh)
vendre _____
to sell

(ray-pay-tay)
répéter _____
to repeat

As always, say each sentence out loud. Say each **et** every **mot** carefully, pronouncing each

French sound as well as **vous** can.

(deer)
dire
to say

Je _dis/_____ "Bonjour."

Vous _dites/_____ *(noh(n))* "Non."
no
(sah-lew)
Il _dit/_____ "Salut."
Elle

Nous _disons/_____ *(wee)* "Oui."

Ils ne _disent/_____ *(rya(n))* rien.
Elles nothing

(koh(n)-prah(n)-druh)
comprendre
to understand

Je _comprends/_____ *(lah(n)-glay)* l'anglais.

Vous _____ *(lee-tah-lya(n))* l'italien.

Il _____ *(lahl-mah(n))* l'allemand.
Elle

Nous _comprenons/_____ *(roos)* le russe.
Russian

Ils _____ le français.
Elles French

(vah(n)-druh)
vendre
to sell

Je _vends/_____ *(day)* des fleurs.
some

Vous ne _____ *(rya(n))* rien.

Il _vend/_____ des cartes postales.
Elle postcards

Nous _____ *(fwee)* du fruit.

Ils _____ *(ta(n)-bruh-pohst)* des timbres-poste.
Elles

(ray-pay-tay)
répéter Que? Que? Que?
to repeat

Je _répète/_____ le mot.

Vous _répétez/_____ la réponse.

Il _répète/_____ *(noh(n))* les noms.
Elle names

Nous _répétons/_____ les questions.
questions

Ils ne _répètent/_____ rien.
Elles

☐ **le pique-nique** *(peek-neek)* .... picnic _____
☐ **la place** *(plahs)*........................ place, seat, square (in a town) _____
☐ **le plaisir** *(play-zeer)* .... pleasure _____
– **Avec plaisir** *(ah-vek)(play-zeer)* .... with pleasure **p** _____
☐ **la police** *(poh-lees)* .... police _____

15 *(ah⁽ⁿ⁾)* *(oh)*
En haut – En bas
above/upstairs   below/downstairs   *(bah)*

(noo) *(zah-loh⁽ⁿ⁾)(ah⁽ⁿ⁾-kor)* *(maze-oh⁽ⁿ⁾)*
Maintenant nous allons encore apprendre des mots. Voilà une maison en France. Go to
    more   learn   house

(shah⁽ⁿ⁾-bruh) *(koo-shay)* *(pyess)* *(noh⁽ⁿ⁾)*
your **chambre à coucher et** look around **la pièce.** Let's learn **les noms** of the things **dans**
bedroom   room   names

(noo)
la chambre, just like **nous** learned the various parts of **la maison.**

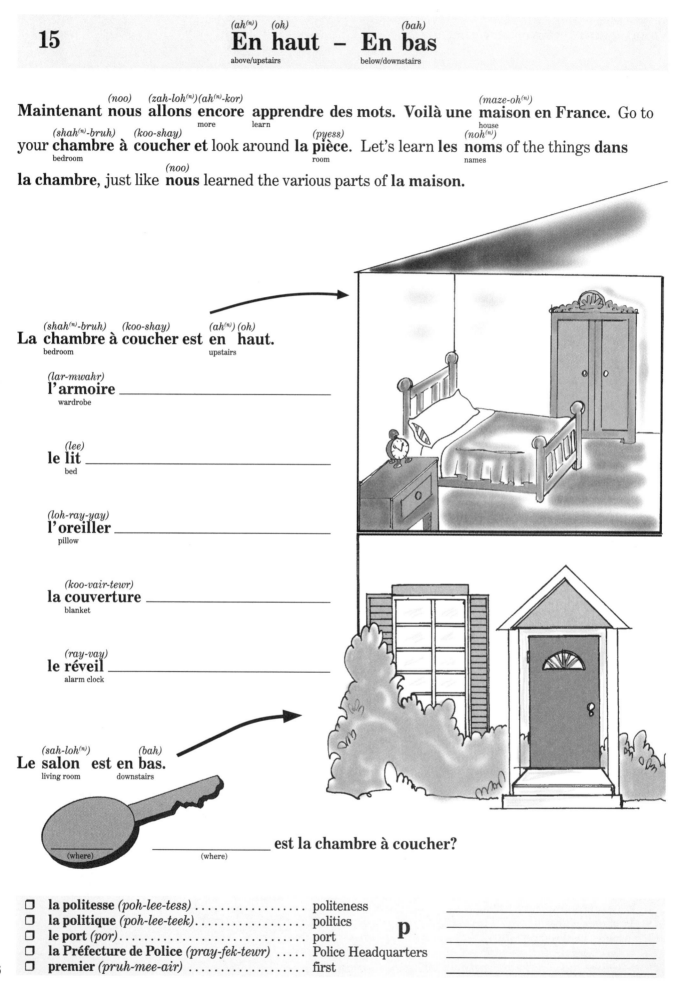

(shah⁽ⁿ⁾-bruh) *(koo-shay)* *(ah⁽ⁿ⁾) (oh)*
La chambre à coucher est en haut.
bedroom   upstairs

(lar-mwahr)
l'armoire _____
wardrobe

(lee)
le lit _____
bed

(loh-ray-yay)
l'oreiller _____
pillow

(koo-vair-tewr)
la couverture _____
blanket

(ray-vay)
le réveil _____
alarm clock

(sah-loh⁽ⁿ⁾) *(bah)*
Le salon est en bas.
living room   downstairs

_____ _____ **est la chambre à coucher?**
(where)   (where)

☐ **la politesse** *(poh-lee-tess)* . . . . politeness
☐ **la politique** *(poh-lee-teek)* . . . . politics
☐ **le port** *(por)* . . . . port   **p** _____
☐ **la Préfecture de Police** *(pray-fek-tewr)* . . . . . Police Headquarters _____
☐ **premier** *(pruh-mee-air)* . . . . first _____

Maintenant, remove the next **cinq** *(sank)* stickers **et** label these things **dans** your **chambre à coucher.**

Let's move into **la salle de bain** *(sahl) (ba⁽ⁿ⁾)* **et** do the same thing. Remember, **la salle de bain** *(ba⁽ⁿ⁾)* means a
bathroom
room to bathe in. If **vous êtes dans un restaurant et vous** *(voo) (zet)* need to use the lavatory, **vous**

want to ask for **les cabinets** *(kah-bee-nay)* **ou les toilettes** *(twah-let)* *not* for **la salle de bain.** Restrooms
or
may be marked with pictures **ou** simply with the letters **D̲ ou M̲.**

Don't confuse them!

D̲ = **Dames** *(dahm)*
ladies' (restroom)

M̲ = **Messieurs** *(mes-syur)*
men's (restroom)

La salle de bain est aussi en haut. *(sahl) (ba⁽ⁿ⁾) (oh-see) (oh)*
bathroom   also

le miroir *(mir-wahr)* _____
mirror

le lavabo *(lah-vah-boh)* _____
washstand

les serviettes *(sair-vyet)* _____
towels

le W.C. *(doo-bul-vay-say)* _____
toilet

la douche *(doosh)* _____
shower

Le bureau est aussi en bas. *(bew-roh) (oh-see) (bah)*
study   also   downstairs

☐ **le président** *(pray-zee-dah⁽ⁿ⁾)* . . . . president
☐ **la presse** *(press)* . . . . press, media
☐ **le prix** *(pree)* . . . . price, prize
☐ **le problème** *(proh-blem)* . . . . problem
☐ **la programme** *(proh-grahm)* . . . . program

p _____
_____
_____
_____
_____

57

Do not forget to remove the next group of stickers **et** label these things in your **maison.** _(may-zoh⁽ⁿ⁾)_ above **maison** Okay,

it is time to review. Here's a quick quiz to see what you remember.

men's (restroom)

(bah)
en bas

I understand

(mes-syur)
messieurs

downstairs

(seel) (voo) (play)
s'il vous plaît

please

(koh⁽ⁿ⁾-prah⁽ⁿ⁾)
je comprends

towels

(sahl) (ba⁽ⁿ⁾)
la salle de bain

upstairs

(too) (dwah)
tout droit

bathroom

(dahm)
dames

lavatory/restroom

(sair-vyet)
les serviettes

straight ahead

_(oh)_
en haut

women's (restroom)

(twah-let)
les toilettes

☐	**le quai** _(kay)_	quay, platform	
☐	**le quartier** _(kar-tee-ay)_	quarter, district	**q**
☐	**quatorze** _(kah-torz)_	fourteen	
	– **Louis Quatorze** _(loo-wee)(kah-torz)_	Louis the Fourteenth	
	– **le quatorze juillet** _(zhwee-ay)_	July 14th-Independence Day	

Next stop — **le bureau,** specifically **la table ou le bureau dans le bureau. Qu'est-ce qu'il y a**
(bew-roh) office · *(tah-bluh)* table · *(bew-roh)* desk · *(kess)* what · *(keel-yah)* is there

sur le bureau? Let's identify **les choses** which one normally finds **sur le bureau** or strewn
on · things

about **la maison.**

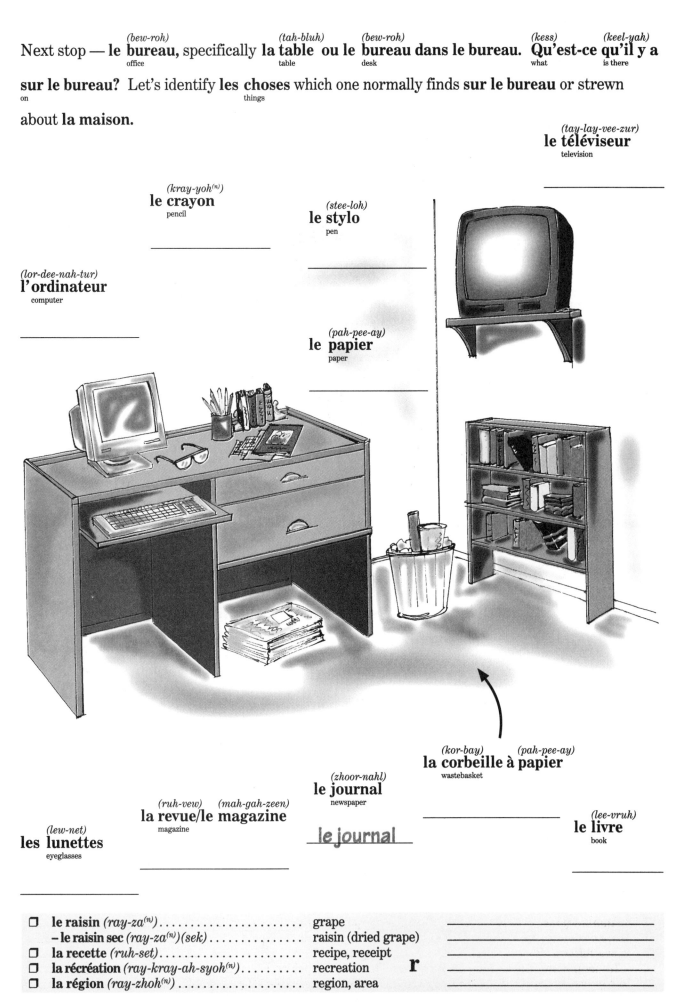

(tay-lay-vee-zur)
le téléviseur
television

(kray-yoh$^{(n)}$)
le crayon
pencil

(stee-loh)
le stylo
pen

(lor-dee-nah-tur)
l'ordinateur
computer

(pah-pee-ay)
le papier
paper

(kor-bay) *(pah-pee-ay)*
la corbeille à papier
wastebasket

(zhoor-nahl)
le journal
newspaper

le journal

(ruh-vew) *(mah-gah-zeen)*
la revue/le magazine
magazine

(lew-net)
les lunettes
eyeglasses

(lee-vruh)
le livre
book

☐ **le raisin** *(ray-za$^{(n)}$)* . . . . grape
– **le raisin sec** *(ray-za$^{(n)}$)(sek)* . . . . raisin (dried grape)
☐ **la recette** *(ruh-set)* . . . . recipe, receipt
☐ **la récréation** *(ray-kray-ah-syoh$^{(n)}$)* . . . . recreation   **r**
☐ **la région** *(ray-zhoh$^{(n)}$)* . . . . region, area

Don't forget these essentials!

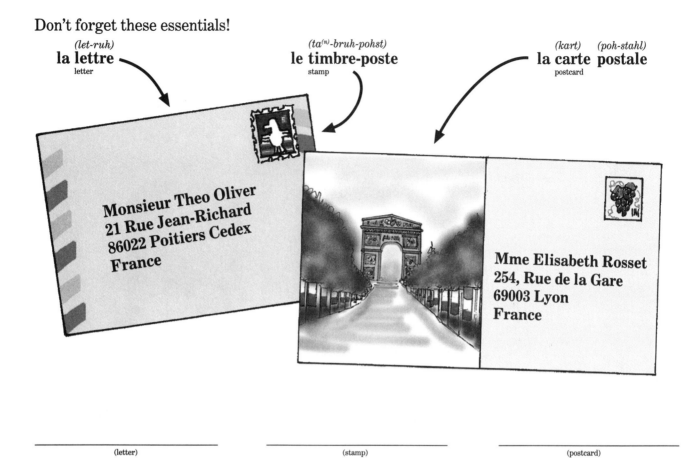

(let-ruh)
la lettre
letter

(ta⁽ⁿ⁾-bruh-pohst)
le timbre-poste
stamp

(kart) *(poh-stahl)*
la carte postale
postcard

Monsieur Theo Oliver
21 Rue Jean-Richard
86022 Poitiers Cedex
France

Mme Elisabeth Rosset
254, Rue de la Gare
69003 Lyon
France

_____ (letter)   _____ (stamp)   _____ (postcard)

Remember that "**oi**" sounds like "wah." Practice this sound **avec les mots suivants**:

(bwah) *(bwah)*   *(ah⁽ⁿ⁾-vwah)* *(ah⁽ⁿ⁾-vwah)*
bois, boit, trois, soixante, mademoiselle, poivre, bonsoir, envoie and **envoient**.
drink   drinks   three   pepper   send   send

(parl) *(parl)* *(mah⁽ⁿ⁾zh)* *(mah⁽ⁿ⁾zh)*
Notice that "**ent**" at the end of a verb is silent: **parle** and **parlent**, **mange** and **mangent**.
speak   speaks   eat   eat

(ness) *(pah)* *(ek-streh-muh-mah⁽ⁿ⁾)*
The expression "**n'est-ce pas**" is **extrêmement** useful **en français**. Added onto a sentence, it
extremely

turns the sentence into a question for which **la réponse** is usually "**oui**." It has only one form

and is much simpler than **en anglais**.

(ness) *(pah)*
C'est un livre, n'est-ce pas?   =   It's a book, isn't it?

(bel)
Jacqueline est belle, n'est-ce pas?   =   Jacqueline is beautiful, isn't she?

(voo) *(zet)*
Vous êtes français, n'est-ce pas?   =   You're French, aren't you?

☐ **la Renaissance** *(ruh-nay-sah⁽ⁿ⁾s)* . . . . rebirth, the Renaissance _____
☐ **le rendez-vous** *(rah⁽ⁿ⁾-day-voo)* . . . . rendezvous, appointment _____
☐ **la république** *(ray-pew-bleek)* . . . . republic   **r** _____
   – **La Cinquième République** (1958-   ) . . . the Fifth Republic _____
☐ **la réservation** *(ray-zair-vah-syoh⁽ⁿ⁾)* . . . . . . reservation _____

Simple, isn't it? **Maintenant**, after you fill in the blanks below, go back a second time and negate all these sentences by adding "**ne**" before each verb and "**pas**" after each verb. Don't get discouraged! Just look at how much **vous** have already learned **et** think ahead to wonderful food, **la Tour** *(toor)* **Eiffel** *(ee-fel)* **et** new adventures.

voir *(vwahr)*
to see
_____

dormir *(dor-meer)*
to sleep
_____

envoyer *(ah(n)-vwhy-ay)*
to send
_____

trouver *(troo-vay)*
to find
_____

---

voir *(vwahr)*
to see

Je _vois/_ _____ le marché. *(mar-shay)* market

Vous _voyez/_ _____ le Louvre. *(loo-vruh)*

Il _voit/_ _____ la Tour Eiffel. *(toor) (ee-fel)*
Elle

Nous _voyons/_ _____ le Pont Neuf. *(poh(n)) (nuf)* bridge

Ils _voient/_ _____ Notre-Dame.
Elles

envoyer *(ah(n)-vwhy-ay)*
to send

J' _envoie/_ _____ la lettre. letter

Vous _envoyez/_ _____ la carte postale.

Il _envoie/_ _____ le livre.
Elle

Nous _____ quatre cartes postales. *(kah-truh)*

Ils _envoient/_ _____ trois lettres.
Elles

dormir *(dor-meer)*
to sleep

Je _dors/_ _____ dans la chambre. *(shah(n)-bruh)*

Vous _dormez/_ _____ dans l'hôtel.

Il _dort/_ _____ dans la maison.
Elle

Nous _____ sous la couverture. *(soo)* blanket

Ils _____ sans les oreillers. *(sah(n))*
Elles without pillows

trouver *(troo-vay)*
to find

Je _____ le Louvre.

Vous _trouvez/_ _____ les lunettes. *(lew-net)*

Il _____ le Musée d'Orsay.
Elle

Nous _____ l'Opéra.

Ils _____ l' Hôtel de Ville. *(veel)*
Elles town hall

☐	la résidence *(ray-zee-dah(n)s)* .... residence	_____
☐	la résistance *(ray-zee-stah(n)s)* .... resistance	_____
☐	la révolution *(ray-voh-lew-syoh(n))* .... revolution **r**	_____
	– 1789 - la Révolution française .... French Revolution	_____
☐	la route *(root)* .... route, highway	_____

Before **vous** proceed with the next step, *(seel) (voo) (play)* **s'il vous plaît,** identify all the items **en bas.**

(zhoor-nahl)
le journal

(kor-bay)
la corbeille à papier

la carte postale

le livre

(ta⁽ⁿ⁾-bruh-pohst)
le timbre-poste

(pah-pee-ay)
le papier

le stylo

(kray-yoh⁽ⁿ⁾)
le crayon

la lettre

(lew-net)
les lunettes

(ruh-vew)
la revue

le téléviseur

(lor-dee-nah-tur)
l'ordinateur

			S	
☐	**le sac** *(sack)*	sack		_____
☐	**sacré** *(sah-kray)*	sacred		_____
	– Sacré-Coeur à Paris *(sah-kray-kur)*	Sacred Heart (church in Paris)		_____
☐	**sage** *(sahzh)*	wise, well-behaved		_____
☐	**la saison** *(say-zoh⁽ⁿ⁾)*	season		_____

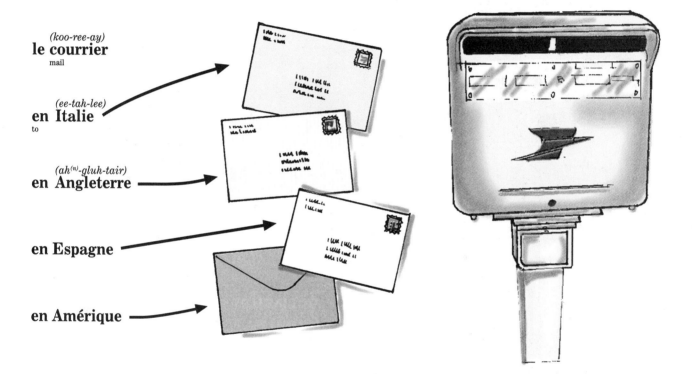

16   **Le Courrier**
(koo-ree-ay)
mail

Maintenant vous know how to count, how to ask **questions**, how to use **verbes avec** the "plug-in"

formula **et** how to describe something, be it the location of **un hôtel ou la couleur d'une maison.**
(dewn)
house

Let's take the basics that **vous** have learned **et** expand them in special areas that will be most

helpful in your travels. What does everyone do on a holiday? Send postcards, **n'est-ce pas?**
(ness) *(pah)*

Let's learn exactly how **le bureau de poste français (P.T.T.)** works.
(bew-roh) *(pohst)* *(pay-tay-tay)*
post office

le courrier
(koo-ree-ay)
mail

en Italie
(ee-tah-lee)
to

en Angleterre
(ah⁽ⁿ⁾-gluh-tair)

en Espagne

en Amérique

Les P.T.T. (**P**ostes, **T**élécommunications et **T**élediffusion) is where **vous** buy **les timbres-**
(lay) *(pay-tay-tay)*

poste, send **les paquets et les cartes postales.** In large cities, **vous** can send **les télégrammes**
(pah-kay) *(tay-lay-grahm)*
packages telegrams

or make **un appel téléphonique interurbain au bureau de poste. Les P.T.T ont tout.**
(ah-pel) *(tay-lay-foh-neek)* *(a⁽ⁿ⁾-tair-ewr-ba⁽ⁿ⁾)* *(ah⁽ⁿ⁾)* *(too)*
long-distance call   at the   have everything

☐ **la salutation** *(sah-lew-tah-syoh⁽ⁿ⁾)*	greeting		_____
☐ **le sandwich** *(sah⁽ⁿ⁾-dweech)*	sandwich		_____
☐ **la sauce** *(sohs)*	sauce	**S**	_____
☐ **le saumon** *(soh-moh⁽ⁿ⁾)*	salmon		_____
☐ **la science** *(see-ah⁽ⁿ⁾s)*	science		_____

Voilà the necessary **mots pour le bureau de poste.** Practice them aloud **et** write them in the blanks.

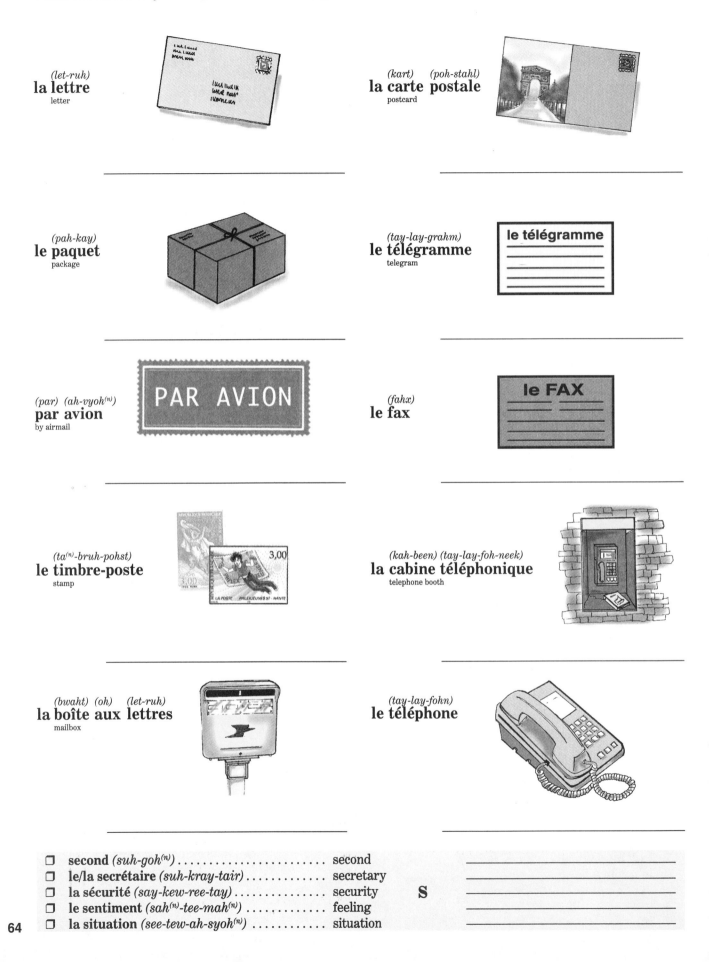

(let-ruh)
la lettre
letter

_____

(kart) *(poh-stahl)*
la carte postale
postcard

_____

(pah-kay)
le paquet
package

_____

(tay-lay-grahm)
le télégramme
telegram

le télégramme

_____

(par) *(ah-vyoh⁽ⁿ⁾)*
par avion
by airmail

PAR AVION

(fahx)
le fax

le FAX

_____

(ta⁽ⁿ⁾-bruh-pohst)
le timbre-poste
stamp

_____

(kah-been) *(tay-lay-foh-neek)*
la cabine téléphonique
telephone booth

_____

(bwaht) *(oh)* *(let-ruh)*
la boîte aux lettres
mailbox

_____

(tay-lay-fohn)
le téléphone

_____

☐ **second** *(suh-goh⁽ⁿ⁾)* . . . . second
☐ **le/la secrétaire** *(suh-kray-tair)* . . . . secretary
☐ **la sécurité** *(say-kew-ree-tay)* . . . . security
☐ **le sentiment** *(sah⁽ⁿ⁾-tee-mah⁽ⁿ⁾)* . . . . feeling
☐ **la situation** *(see-tew-ah-syoh⁽ⁿ⁾)* . . . . situation

S

_____

_____

_____

_____

_____

64

Next step — **vous** ask **questions** like those **en bas**, depending on what **vous** **voudriez.** $^{(voo\text{-}dree\text{-}ay)}$ Repeat

these sentences aloud many times.

(oo) (ess) (koh$^{(n)}$) (nah-shet)
Où est-ce qu'on achète des timbres-poste? _____
does   one   buy

Où est-ce qu'on achète une carte postale? _____

(koh$^{(n)}$) (tay-lay-fohn)
Où est-ce qu'on téléphone? _____
does   one   telephone

(ay) (bwaht) (oh)
Où est la boîte aux lettres? _____
is

(ay) (kah-been) (tay-lay-foh-neek)
Où est la cabine téléphonique? _____
is

(ess) (koh$^{(n)}$) (nah$^{(n)}$-vwah)
Où est-ce qu'on envoie un paquet? _____
does   one   send

(fay) (ah-pel)
Où est-ce qu'on fait un appel téléphonique? _____
make   call

(kohm-bya$^{(n)}$) (ess) (kuh) (sah)(koot)
Combien est-ce que ça coûte? _____ *Combien est-ce que ça coûte?* _____

Maintenant, quiz yourself. See if **vous** can translate the following thoughts **en français.**

1. Where is the telephone booth? _____

2. Where does one make a telephone call? _____

3. Where does one make a local telephone call? _____

4. Where is the post office? _____

5. Where does one buy stamps? _____

6. How much is it? _____

7. Where does one send a package? _____

8. Where does one send a fax? _____

Voilà quatre nouveaux verbes.

(fair)
faire _____
to make, to do

(moh⁽ⁿ⁾-tray)
montrer _____
to show

(ay-kreer)
écrire _____
to write

(pay-yay)
payer _____
to pay

Practice these verbs by not only filling in the blanks, but by saying them aloud many, many

times until you are comfortable with the sounds **et** the words.

(fair)
faire
to make, to do

Je _fais/_____ le **lit.** *(lee)*
bed

Vous _faites/_____ **un appel téléphonique.**

Il _fait/_____ **beaucoup.** *(boh-koo)*
Elle   a lot

Nous ne _faisons/_____ **rien.** *(rya⁽ⁿ⁾)*
nothing

Ils _font/_____ **tout.** *(too)*
Elles   everything

(ay-kreer)
écrire
to write

J' _écris/_____ l' **adresse.** *(lah-dress)*
address

Vous _écrivez/_____ **votre nom.** *(voh-truh) (noh⁽ⁿ⁾)*
your

Il n' _écrit/_____ **rien.** *(lah-dress)*
Elle   nothing

Nous _écrivons/_____ **beaucoup.**
a lot

Ils _écrivent/_____ **un fax.** *(fahx)*
Elles

(moh⁽ⁿ⁾-tray)
montrer
to show

Je vous _montre/_____ **le livre.** *(voo)*
to you

Vous me _____ **la lettre.** *(muh)*
to me

Il vous _____ **le château.** *(shah-toh)*
Elle   castle

Nous vous _____ **l'hôtel.** *(voo)*
to you

Ils me _____ **les P.T.T.** *(muh)* *(pay-tay-tay)*
Elles

(pay-yay)
payer
to pay

Je _paie/_____ **la note.** *(noht)*
bill in hotel

Vous _payez/_____ **la taxe.** *(tahx)*
tax

Il _paie/_____ **l'addition.** *(lah-dee-syoh⁽ⁿ⁾)*
Elle   bill in a restaurant

Nous ne _payons/_____ **rien.**

Ils _paient/_____ **le prix.** *(pree)*
Elles   price

☐ **le ski** *(ski)* .... skiing
– **le ski-nautique** *(ski-noh-teek)* .... water skiing   **S** _____
☐ **la Sorbonne** *(sor-bun)* .... part of University of Paris _____
☐ **la soupe** *(soup)* .... soup _____
☐ **le spectacle** *(spek-tah-kluh)* .... spectacle, performance _____

Some of these signs you probably recognize, but take a couple of minutes to review them anyway.

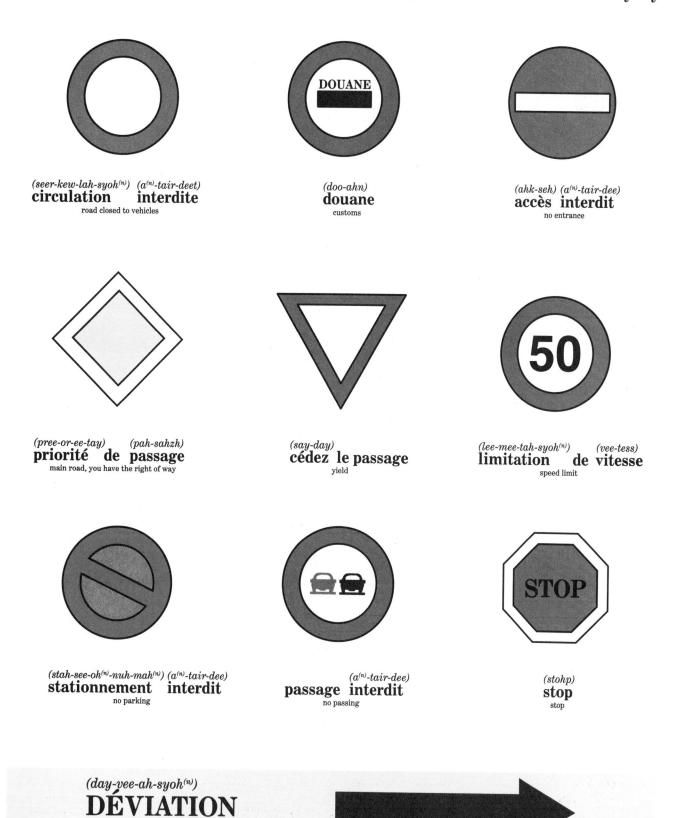

(seer-kew-lah-syoh[n]) *(a[n]-tair-deet)*
circulation   **interdite**
road closed to vehicles

(doo-ahn)
douane
customs

(ahk-seh) *(a[n]-tair-dee)*
accès **interdit**
no entrance

(pree-or-ee-tay) *(pah-sahzh)*
priorité **de** **passage**
main road, you have the right of way

(say-day)
cédez **le passage**
yield

(lee-mee-tah-syoh[n]) *(vee-tess)*
limitation **de** **vitesse**
speed limit

(stah-see-oh[n]-nuh-mah[n]) *(a[n]-tair-dee)*
stationnement **interdit**
no parking

(a[n]-tair-dee)
passage **interdit**
no passing

(stohp)
stop
stop

(day-vee-ah-syoh[n])
DÉVIATION
detour

What follows are approximate conversions, so when you order something by liters, kilograms or grams you will have an idea of what to expect and not find yourself being handed one piece of candy when you thought you ordered an entire bag.

To Convert		Do the Math		
liters (l) to gallons, gallons to liters,	multiply by 0.26 multiply by 3.79	4 liters x 0.26 10 gal. x 3.79	= =	1.04 gallons 37.9 liters
kilograms (kg) to pounds, pounds to kilos,	multiply by 2.2 multiply by 0.46	2 kilograms x 2.2 10 pounds x 0.46	= =	4.4 pounds 4.6 kg
grams (g) to ounces, ounces to grams,	multiply by 0.035 multiply by 28.35	100 grams x 0.035 10 oz. x 28.35	= =	3.5 oz. 283.5 g.
meters (m) to feet, feet to meters,	multiply by 3.28 multiply by 0.3	2 meters x 3.28 6 feet x 0.3	= =	6.56 feet 1.8 meters

For fun, take your weight in pounds and convert it into kilograms. It sounds better that way, doesn't it? How many kilometers is it from your home to school, to work, to the post office?

The Simple Versions		
one liter	=	approximately one US quart
four liters	=	approximately one US gallon
one kilo	=	approximately 2.2 pounds
100 grams	=	approximately 3.5 ounces
500 grams	=	slightly more than one pound
one meter	=	slightly more than three feet

The distance between **New York et Paris** is approximately 3,622 miles. How many kilometers would that be? It is 215 miles between **Londres et Paris**. How many kilometers is that?

kilometers (km.) to miles, miles to kilometers,	multiply by 0.62 multiply by 1.6	1000 km. x 0.62 1000 miles x 1.6	= =	620 miles 1,600 km.

Inches	1	2	3	4	5	6	7

To convert centimeters into inches, multiply by 0.39   Example: 9 cm. x 0.39 = 3.51 in.

To convert inches into centimeters, multiply by 2.54   Example: 4 in. x 2.54 = 10.16 cm.

cm 1	2	3	4	5	6	7	8	9	10	11	12	13	14	15	16	17	18

(koh-mah⁽ⁿ⁾) *(pay-yay)*

Comment Payer
how — to pay

Oui, il y a aussi bills to pay en France. Vous have just finished your *(ruh-pah) (day-lee-syuh)* **repas délicieux et**
(eel-yah) *(oh-see)* — there are — also — meal — delicious

vous voudriez l'addition. Que faites-vous? Vous call for **le serveur (le garçon) ou la**
(voo-dree-ay) *(lah-dee-syoh⁽ⁿ⁾)* *(fet-voo)* *(sair-vur)* *(gar-soh⁽ⁿ⁾)*
would like — bill — do you do — waiter

serveuse. Le serveur will normally reel off what **vous avez** eaten while writing rapidly. **Il** will
(sair-vuz) *(zah-vay)*
waitress — have

then place a piece **de papier sur la table, et** say, "Ça fait soixante francs." **Vous** will pay **le**
(fay)
makes

serveur ou perhaps **vous** will pay **à la caisse.**
(kess)
cashier

If your bill or the menu is marked "**service compris**," then your tip has already been included in
(sair-vees) *(koh⁽ⁿ⁾-pree)*
included

your bill. If the service is not included in **l'addition**, round the bill up **ou** simply leave what you

consider an appropriate amount for your **serveur sur la table.** When **vous** dine out on your

voyage, it is always a good idea to make a reservation. It can be difficult to get into a popular
(vwah-yahzh)
trip

restaurant. Nevertheless, the experience is well worth the trouble **vous** might encounter to
(reh-stoh-rah⁽ⁿ⁾)

obtain a reservation. **Et** remember, **vous savez** enough **français** to make a reservation. Just
(sah-vay)
know

speak slowly and clearly. This is a good phrase to know:

(eel) (nyah) (pah) (kwah)
*Il n'y a pas de quoi.
it is nothing/you're welcome

❏	**le sport** *(spor)*	sport	_____
❏	**stopper** *(stoh-pay)*	to stop	_____
❏	**stupide** *(stew-peed)*	stupid	**S** _____
❏	**la Suède** *(swed)*	Sweden	_____
❏	**la Suisse** *(swees)*	Switzerland	_____

Remember these key **mots** when dining out **à la française.**
(frah⁽ⁿ⁾-sez)
in the French manner

(sair-vur) *(gar-soh⁽ⁿ⁾)*
le serveur/le garçon _____
waiter

(sair-vuz)
la serveuse _____
waitress

(lah-dee-syoh⁽ⁿ⁾)
l' addition *l'addition, l'addition*
bill

(poor-bwahr)
le pourboire _____
tip

(muh-new) *(kart)*
le menu/ la carte _____
menu

(eel)(nyah) *(pah)(duh)(kwah)*
il n'y a pas de quoi _____
it's nothing/you're welcome

(ek-skew-zay-mwah)
excusez-moi _____
excuse me

(mair-see)
merci _____
thank you

(seel) (voo) (play)
s'il vous plaît _____
please

(doh⁽ⁿ⁾-nay-mwah)
donnez-moi . . . _____
give me

Voilà une sample **conversation** involving paying **la note** when leaving **un hôtel.**
(koh⁽ⁿ⁾-vair-sah-syoh⁽ⁿ⁾) *(noht)*
bill

Jeannette: **Excusez-moi. Je voudrais payer la note.**
(voo-dray) *(pay-yay)*
to pay

_____ *Excusez-moi. Je voudrais payer la note.*

(loh-tel-yay)
L'Hôtelier: **Quelle chambre, s'il vous plaît?**
hotelkeeper   *(kel)*
which   room

_____

Jeannette: **Numéro trois cent dix.**
(noo-may-roh)
number

_____

L'Hôtelier: **Merci. Une minute, s'il vous plaît.**

_____

L'Hôtelier: **Voilà la note.**

_____

If **vous** have any problems **avec les nombres,** just ask someone to write out **la somme,** so that
(sohm)
sum

vous can be sure you understand everything correctly,

"**S'il vous plaît,** *écrivez-moi* **la somme. Merci.**"
(ay-kree-vay-mwah)
please   write   for me

Practice: _____
(Please write the sum for me. Thank you.)

❑ **supérieur** *(syoo-pay-ree-ur)* . . . . superior, upper _____
❑ **la surprise** *(sewr-preez)* . . . . surprise _____
❑ **sympathique** *(sa⁽ⁿ⁾-pah-teek)* . . . . likeable, nice   **S** _____
– **Qu'il est sympa!** *(keel)(ay)(sa⁽ⁿ⁾-pah)* . . . . Oh, he's so nice. _____
❑ **la système** *(see-stem)* . . . . system _____

70

Maintenant, let's take a break from **les additions et l'argent** *(lar-zhah⁽ⁿ⁾)* et learn some fun **nouveaux**

money — new

mots. Vous can always practice these **mots** by using your flash cards at the back of this **livre.**

Carry these flash cards in your purse, pocket, briefcase **ou** knapsack **et** *use them!*

(oo-vair)
ouvert
open

_____

(fair-may)
fermé
closed

_____

(grah⁽ⁿ⁾)
grand
big

_____

(puh-tee)
petit
small

_____

(bun) *(sah⁽ⁿ⁾-tay)*
en bonne santé
healthy

_____

(mah-lahd)
malade
sick

_____

(boh⁽ⁿ⁾)
bon
good

_____

(moh-vay)
mauvais
bad

_____

(shoh)
chaud
hot

_____

(fwah)
froid
cold

_____

☐ **le tabac** *(tah-bah)* . . . . tobacco _____
– **le bureau de tabac** *(bew-roh)(duh)(tah-bah)* . . tobacco shop _____
☐ **la tapisserie** *(tah-pee-suh-ree)* . . . . tapestry, wallpaper **t** _____
☐ **le tarif** *(tah-reef)* . . . . tariff, fare _____
☐ **le tennis** *(teh-nees)* . . . . tennis _____

(koor)
court
short

(lohng)
long
long

(lah⁽ⁿ⁾)

(lah^{(n)})
lent
slow

(veet) (rah-peed)
vite/rapide
fast

(grah^{(n)}) (oh)
grand/haut
tall   high

(puh-tee) (bah)
petit/ bas
short   low

(vee-yuh)
vieux
old

(zhun)
jeune
young

(shair)
cher
expensive

(boh^{(n)}) (mar-shay)
bon marché
inexpensive

(reesh)
riche
rich

(poh-vruh)
pauvre
poor

(boh-koo)
beaucoup
a lot

(puh)
peu
a little

☐	**la terrasse** *(tay-rahs)*	terrace, sidewalk cafe	
☐	**thermal** *(tair-mahl)*	thermal	
	– **les eaux thermales** *(lay)(zoh)(tair-mahl)* . .	hot springs	**t**
☐	**le théâtre** *(tay-ah-truh)*	theater	
☐	**le ticket** *(tee-kay)*	ticket	

Voilà des nouveaux verbes.
some

(sah-vwahr)
savoir _____
to know (fact, address)

(leer)
lire _____
to read

(poo-vwahr)
pouvoir _____
to be able to, can

(duh-vwahr)
devoir _____
to have to, must, to owe

Study the patterns below closely, as **vous** will use these verbs a lot.

Rue de Varenne

Je sais l'adresse.

(sah-vwahr)
savoir
to know

Je _sais/_____ tout.
everything

Vous _savez/_____ l'adresse.
address

Il _sait/_____ parler français.
Elle
to speak

Nous _savons/_____ le nom de l'hôtel.
name

Ils ne _savent/_____ pas l'adresse.
Elles

(poo-vwahr)
pouvoir
to be able to, can

Je _peux/_____ commander un café.

(ah-shuh-tay)
Vous _pouvez/_____ acheter un journal.

(ah⁽ⁿ⁾-vwah-yay)
Il _peut/_____ envoyer une lettre.
Elle
read

(mah⁽ⁿ⁾-zhay)
Nous _pouvons/_____ manger au restaurant.

(pay-yay) *(noht)*
Ils _peuvent/_____ payer la note.
Elles
bill (hotel)

(leer)
lire
to read

Je _lis/_____ le livre.

(ruh-vew)
Vous _lisez/_____ la revue.
magazine

Il _lit/_____ le menu.
Elle

Nous _lisons/_____ beaucoup.
a lot
(zhoor-nahl)
Ils _lisent/_____ le journal.
Elles
newspaper

(duh-vwahr)
devoir
to have to, must, to owe

(ah-prah⁽ⁿ⁾-druh)
Je _dois/_____ apprendre le français.

(leer)
Vous _devez/_____ lire le livre.

(reh-stay)
Il _doit/_____ rester à l'hôtel.
Elle
remain

(vee-zee-tay)
Nous _devons/_____ visiter Paris.
visit
(pay-yay)
Ils _doivent/_____ payer l'addition.
Elles

❑ **la tour** *(tour)*	tower	_____
❑ **le tour** *(tour)*	circumference, tour	_____
– **Le Tour de France**	bicycle race in France **t**	_____
❑ **tricolore** *(tree-koh-lor)*	tricolored	_____
– **le drapeau tricolore** *(drah-poh)* . .	French flag (**bleu, blanc, rouge**)	_____

73

Notice that "**pouvoir**," "**devoir**," et "**savoir**" along with "**voudrais**" and "**voudrions**" can be combined

with another verb.

(say) Je **sais** trouver l'adresse. know how to find	*(poo-voh(n))* *(reh-stay)* Nous **pouvons** rester à Paris. can	*(dwah)* Elle **doit** dormir. must/has to sleep
(say) *(koh(n)-mah(n)-day)* Je **sais** commander une bière. to order	*(ah(n)-vwah-yay)* *(let-ruh)* Nous pouvons envoyer une lettre.	Elle doit payer l'addition.

(say) *(par-lay)*
Je **sais** parler français.
I   know how
(puh)
Je **peux** commander un livre.
can
(dwah)
Je **dois** parler français.
must
(voo-dray)
Je **voudrais** parler français.
would like

(poo-vay-voo)
Pouvez-vous translate the sentences **en français?** **Les réponses sont en bas.**
can

1. I know how to speak French. _____

2. They can pay the bill. _____

3. He has to pay the bill. _____

4. We know the answers. _____ Nous savons les réponses. _____

5. She knows a lot. _____

6. We know how to read French. _____

7. I cannot find the hotel. _____

8. We are not able to (cannot) understand French. _____

9. I would like to visit Lyon. _____

10. She reads the newspaper. _____

RÉPONSES

10. Elle lit le journal.		
9. Je voudrais visiter Lyon.	5. Elle sait beaucoup.	
8. Nous ne pouvons pas comprendre le français.	4. Nous savons les réponses.	
7. Je ne peux pas trouver l'hôtel.	3. Il doit payer l'addition.	
6. Nous savons lire le français.	2. Ils peuvent payer l'addition.	
	1. Je sais parler français.	

Maintenant, draw **des lignes** *(leen-yuh)* **entre** the opposites **en bas.** Do not forget to say them out loud.

Say **ces mots** *(say)* every day to describe **les choses dans votre** *(voh-truh)* **maison, dans votre école ou dans** *(ay-kohl)*

votre bureau.

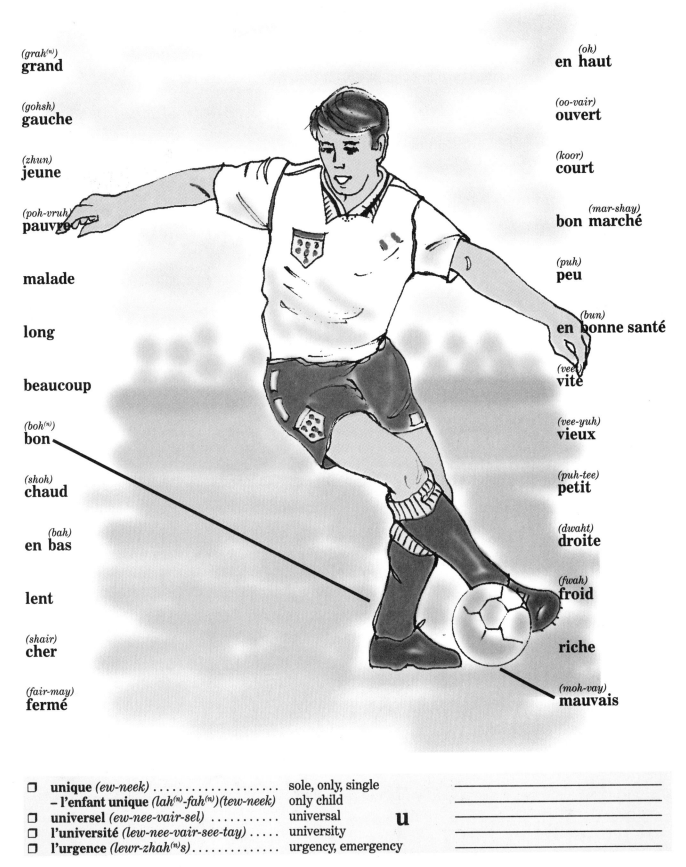

(grah⁽ⁿ⁾)
grand

(gohsh)
gauche

(zhun)
jeune

(poh-vruh)
pauvre

malade

long

beaucoup

(boh⁽ⁿ⁾)
bon

(shoh)
chaud

(bah)
en bas

lent

(shair)
cher

(fair-may)
fermé

(oh)
en haut

(oo-vair)
ouvert

(koor)
court

(mar-shay)
bon marché

(puh)
peu

(bun)
en bonne santé

(veet)
vite

(vee-yuh)
vieux

(puh-tee)
petit

(dwaht)
droite

(fwah)
froid

riche

(moh-vay)
mauvais

☐ **unique** *(ew-neek)* . . . . sole, only, single _____
  – **l'enfant unique** *(lah⁽ⁿ⁾-fah⁽ⁿ⁾)(tew-neek)* only child _____
☐ **universel** *(ew-nee-vair-sel)* . . . . universal **u** _____
☐ **l'université** *(lew-nee-vair-see-tay)* . . . . . university _____
☐ **l'urgence** *(lewr-zhah⁽ⁿ⁾s)* . . . . urgency, emergency _____

75

Le **Voyageur** **Voyage**
(vwah-yah-zhur) *(vwah-yahzh)*
traveler   travels

(ee-air)
Hier à Bordeaux!
yesterday

(oh-zhoor-dwee)
Aujourd'hui à Tours!
today

(duh-ma$^{(n)}$)
Demain à Nice!
tomorrow

If you know a few key **mots,** traveling can be easy in most French-speaking countries. **La**

(nay) *(pah)*
France n'est pas très grande, in fact, it is slightly smaller than the state of Texas. **Donc, c'est**
is not *(doh$^{(n)}$k)*
(fah-seel) therefore
très facile voyager in France. **Comment est-ce que vous voyagez en France?**
easy *(ess)*

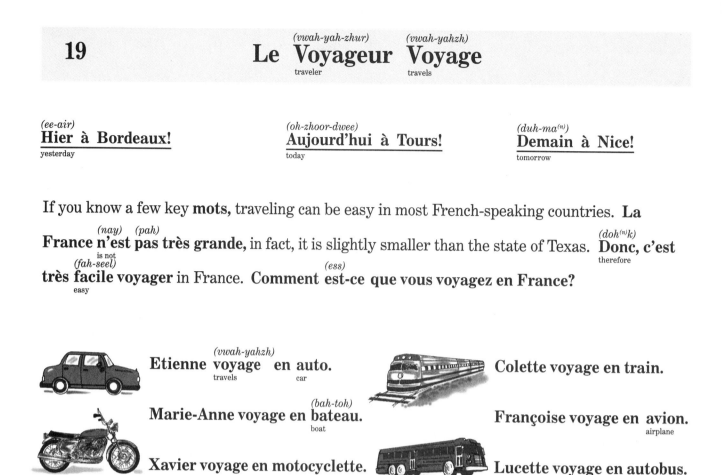

(vwah-yahzh)
Etienne voyage en auto.
travels   car

Colette voyage en train.

(bah-toh)
Marie-Anne voyage en bateau.
boat

Françoise voyage en avion.
airplane

Xavier voyage en motocyclette.

Lucette voyage en autobus.

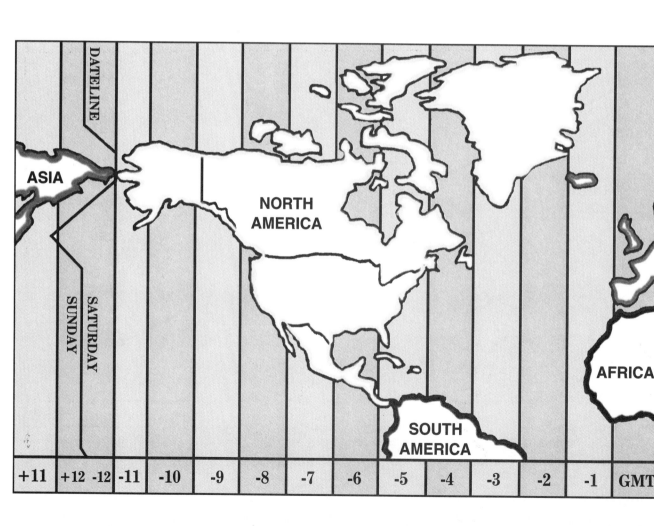

Quand vous are traveling, **vous** will want to tell others your nationality **et vous** will meet people from all corners of the world. Can you guess where people are from if they say one of the following? **Les réponses** are in your glossary beginning on page 108.

(vya⁽ⁿ⁾) *(dah⁽ⁿ⁾-gluh-tair)*
Je viens d'Angleterre. _____
come   from

(dee-tah-lee)
Je viens d'Italie. _____

(day) (zay-tah-zoo-nee)
Je viens des États-Unis. _____

(deh-spahn-yuh)
Je viens d'Espagne. _____

(bel-zheek)
Je viens de Belgique. _____

(swees)
Je viens de Suisse. _____

(mah-rohk)
Je viens du Maroc. _____

(day-kohs)
Je viens d'Écosse. _____

(doh-treesh)
Je viens d'Autriche. _____

(noo) *(vuh-noh⁽ⁿ⁾)* *(roo-see)*
Nous venons de Russie. _____
we   come

(dahl-mahn-yuh)
Nous venons d'Allemagne. _____

(dees-rah-el)
Nous venons d'Israël. _____

(tew-nee-zee)
Nous venons de Tunisie. _____

(dahl-zhay-ree)
Il vient d'Algérie. _____
he   comes

(deer-lahnd)
Il vient d'Irelande. _____

(por-too-gahl)
Elle vient du Portugal. _____
she   comes

(dah-freek)
Elle vient d'Afrique du Sud. _____

Je viens du Canada. _____

EUROPE

ASIA

AFRICA

DATELINE

SATURDAY
SUNDAY

-1	GMT	+1	+2	+3	+4	+5	+6	+7	+8	+9	+10	+11	+12 -12

Le mot for "trip" is taken from **le mot** "**voyager**," *(vwah-yah-zhay)* (to travel) which makes it easy: **voyage**. *(vwah-yahzh)* (trip) **Beaucoup de mots** revolve around the concept of travel which is exactly what **vous voudriez faire**. Practice the following **mots** many times. **Vous** will see them often.

(vwah-yah-zhay)
voyager _____
to travel

(ah-zhah[n]s)   (vwah-yahzh)
une agence de voyage _____
travel agency

(vwah-yah-zhur)
le voyageur _____
traveler

(boh[n])
Bon voyage! _____
have a good trip

If **vous** choose **aller en automobile**, *(ah-lay)* (to go) **voilà** a few key **mots**.

(loh-toh-root)
l'autoroute _____
freeway

(vwah-tewr)   (loo-ay)
une voiture à louer _____
rental car

(root)
la route _____
road

(ah-zhah[n]s)   (loh-kah-syoh[n])   (vwah-tewr)
une agence de location   de voitures _____
car-rental agency

(koh[n]-trah-vah[n]-syoh[n])
une contravention _____
parking ticket

(stah-syoh[n])   (day-sah[n]s)
la station   d'essence _____
service station

En bas il y a *(eel-yah)* (there are) some basic signs which **vous** should **aussi** *(oh-see)* learn to recognize quickly.

(ah[n]-tray)
entrer _____
to enter

(sor-teer)
sortir _____
to exit

ENTRÉE

SORTIE

(lah[n]-tray)
l'entrée _____
entrance

(sor-tee)
la sortie _____
exit

l'entrée principale *(pra[n]-see-pahl)* (main) _____

la sortie de secours *(suh-koor)* _____
emergency exit

POUSSEZ

TIREZ

(poo-say)
poussez _____
push (doors)

(tee-ray)
tirez _____
pull (doors)

❑	**les vacances** *(vah-kah[n]s)*	vacation, holidays	_____
	– **les grandes vacances**	summer vacation	
❑	**la valse** *(vahls)*	waltz **v**	_____
❑	**la vanille** *(vah-nee-yuh)*	vanilla	_____
	– **la glace à la vanille** *(glahs)*	vanilla ice cream	_____

Let's learn the basic travel verbs. Take out a piece of paper **et** make up your own sentences with these **nouveaux mots.** Follow the same pattern **vous** have in previous Steps.

(vwah-yah-zhay) *(ah-vyoh⁽ⁿ⁾)*
voyager en avion _____
to fly

(ah-ree-vay)
arriver _____
to arrive

(sor-teer)
sortir _____
to leave

(eel-yah)
il y a _____
there is, there are

(ah-lay)
aller _____
to go

(par-teer)
partir _____
to depart (vehicles)

(fair) *(vah-leez)*
faire la valise _____
to pack   suitcase

(shah⁽ⁿ⁾-zhay) *(tra⁽ⁿ⁾)*
changer de train _____
to transfer (trains)

Voilà des nouveaux mots pour votre voyage.
     some

(lah-ay-roh-por)
l' aéroport
airport

(kay)
le quai
platform

(loh-rair)
l' horaire
timetable

DE PARIS À TOURS		
Départ	**Nº de train**	**Arrivée**
00:41	50	09:41
07:40	19	16:40
12:15	22	21:15
14:32	10	23:32
21:40	04	06:40

(gar)
la gare
train station

❏ **la variété** *(vah-ree-ay-tay)* . . . . variety
❏ **la veine** *(ven)* . . . . vein (in the body)
  – **avoir de la veine** *(ah-vwahr)(duh)(lah)(ven)* . . to be lucky **V**
❏ **la version** *(vair-syoh⁽ⁿ⁾)* . . . . version
  – **la version originale (VO)** *(oh-ree-zhee-nahl)* . . original version (of a film)

_____
_____
_____
_____
_____

Avec ces mots, vous *(voo)* êtes *(zet)* ready for any **voyage**, anywhere. **Vous** should have no **problèmes avec**

these verbs, just remember the basic "plug-in" formula **vous** have already learned. Use that

knowledge to translate the following thoughts **en français. Les réponses sont en bas.**
into

1. I fly to Paris. ———————————————————————————

2. I transfer trains in Toulon. ————————————————————

3. He goes to Marseille. ——— Il va à Marseille. Il va à Marseille. ————

4. We arrive tomorrow. —————————————————————

5. We buy three tickets to Tours. ———————————————————

6. They travel to Strasbourg. ——————————————————

7. Where is the train to Bordeaux? ————————————————

8. How can we fly to Switzerland? With Swiss Air or with Air France? ————————

Voilà some **mots importants pour le voyageur.**
traveler

DE PARIS À TOURS		
Départ	**Nº de train**	**Arrivée**
00:41	50	09:41
07:40	19	16:40
12:15	22	21:15
14:32	10	23:32
21:40	04	06:40

(oh-kew-pay)
occupé ————————————
occupied

(day-par)
le départ ————————————
departure

(lee-bruh)
libre ————————————
free

(lah-ree-vay)
l'arrivée ————————————
arrival

(koh(n)-par-tuh-mah(n))
le compartiment ————————————
compartment, wagon

(lay-trah(n)-zhay)
à l'étranger ————————————
abroad

(plahs)
la place ————————————
seat

(la(n)-tay-ree-ur)
à l'intérieur ————————————
domestic, internal (of the country)

Increase your travel **mots** by writing out **les mots en bas et** practicing the sample **phrases** *(frahz)* sentences

out loud. Practice asking **questions avec "où."** It will help you later.

(poor)
pour _____
for
Où est le train pour Paris?

(port)
la porte _____
gate
Où est la porte numéro 5?

(day) (zohb-zhay)(troo-vay)
le bureau des objets trouvés _____
lost-and-found office
Y a-t-il un bureau des objets trouvés?

(por-tur)
le porteur _____ *Où est le porteur? Où est le porteur?*
porter
Où est le porteur?

(vohl)
le vol _____
flight
Où est le vol pour Marseille?

(koh$^{(n)}$-seen-yuh)
la consigne _____
left-luggage office
Y a-t-il une consigne?

(bew-roh)   (shah$^{(n)}$zh)
le bureau de change _____
money-exchange office
Où est le bureau de change?

(ghee-shay)
le guichet _____
counter
Où est le guichet numéro sept?

(sahl)   (dah-tah$^{(n)}$t)
la salle d'attente _____
waiting room
Y a-t-il une salle d'attente?

(vah-goh$^{(n)}$-reh-stoh-rah$^{(n)}$)
le wagon-restaurant _____
dining car
Y a-t-il un wagon-restaurant dans le train?

(vah-goh$^{(n)}$-lee)
le wagon-lit _____
sleeping car
Y a-t-il un wagon-lit dans le train?

(koo-shet)
la couchette _____
berth, bunk
Y a-t-il des couchettes dans le train?

_____ _____ *(par)* **part le train?**
(when)   (when)

_____ _____ *(key) (suh)(pahs)* **est-ce qui se passe?**
(what)   (what)   is happening

☐ **la vierge** *(vee-airzh)* . . . . virgin _____
– **la Sainte Vierge** *(sa$^{(n)}$t)(vee-airzh)* . . . . Virgin Mary _____
☐ **la vigne** *(veen-yuh)* . . . . grape vine   **v** _____
☐ **le vigneron** *(veen-yur-oh$^{(n)}$)* . . . . wine-grower _____
☐ **le vignoble** *(veen-yoh-bluh)* . . . . vineyard _____

Pouvez-vous lire les _(frahz)_ phrases suivantes?
can   read   following

Vous êtes maintenant assis dans l'avion _(voo)_ _(zet)_ _(ah-see)_
seated

et vous voyagez en France. Vous avez _(voo)_ _(zah-vay)_

de l'argent, votre billet, votre passeport

et vos valises. Vous êtes maintenant _(voh)_ _(vah-leez)_
your   suitcases

touriste. Vous arrivez demain à 14:15 en

France. Bon voyage! Amusez-vous

bien. _(bya⁽ⁿ⁾)_
well

En France il y a _(eel-yah)_ many different types of trains – **l'omnibus et l'autorail sont lents; le rapide** _(lohm-nee-boos)_ _(loh-toh-rye)_ _(lah⁽ⁿ⁾)_ _(rah-peed)_
there are

et l'express _(lek-spress)_ are much faster. If **vous** plan to travel a long distance, **vous** may wish to catch an

Inter-City train or **TGV (<u>t</u>rain à <u>g</u>rande <u>v</u>itesse)** which travels faster **et** makes fewer

intermediate stops.

❏ **le village** _(vee-lahzh)_	village		
❏ **le vin** _(va⁽ⁿ⁾)_	wine		
❏ **la visite** _(vee-zeet)_	visit	**v**	
❏ **la vitamine** _(vee-tah-meen)_	vitamin		
❏ **le vocabulaire** _(voh-kah-bew-lair)_	vocabulary		

82

Knowing these travel **mots** will make your holiday twice as enjoyable **et** at least three times as easy. Review these **mots** by doing the crossword puzzle **en bas**. Drill yourself on this Step by selecting other destinations **et** ask your own **questions** about **les trains, les autobus et les avions** that go there. Select more **nouveaux mots de votre dictionnaire et** ask your own questions beginning with **quand, où et combien**. **Les réponses** to the crossword puzzle are at the bottom of the next page.

ACROSS

1. money
2. train station
3. timetable
4. to pay
5. occupied
6. counter, window
7. we
8. with
9. lost-and-found office
10. no
11. airport
12. free (unoccupied)
13. to go
14. passport
15. entrance

DOWN

1. to arrive
2. thank you
3. to change trains
4. waiting room
5. traveler
6. dining car
7. have a good trip
8. platform
9. to know (a fact)
11. she
12. to leave
13. weather, time
14. seat
15. exit
16. nothing

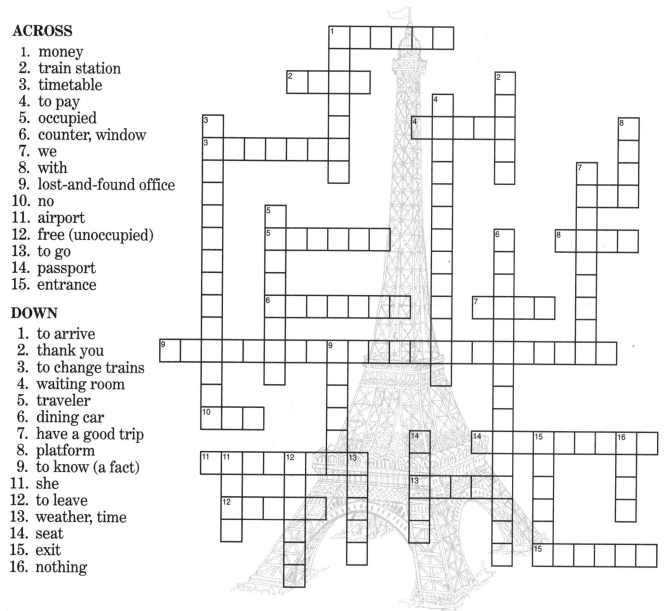

Eiffel Tower – La Tour Eiffel is Paris' most famous landmark. It was first opened in 1889 and soars to a height of over 1,000 feet.

Most "w" words are foreign additions to **le français**.

☐ **le wagon** *(vah-goh⁽ⁿ⁾)* . . . . railroad car		_____
☐ **le week-end** *(week-end)* . . . . weekend	**W**	_____
☐ **le western** *(wes-tairn)* . . . . western (film)		_____
☐ **le whisky** *(wee-skee)* . . . . whisky		_____

What about inquiring about **le prix des billets ou le tarif?** *(pree)* *(bee-ay)* *(tah-reef)* **Vous pouvez** ask these **questions.**

Combien est le tarif pour Lille? *(kohm-bya⁽ⁿ⁾)* *(leel)* _____

Combien est le billet pour Bayonne? *(by-ohn)* _____

Combien est le billet pour Bourdeaux? *(bor-doh)* _____

aller *(ah-lay)* _____
one-way

aller et retour *(ah-lay) (ruh-tour)* _____
round-trip

What about times of **départs et arrivées?** *(day-par) (ah-ree-vay)* **Vous pouvez** ask **ces questions aussi.**
departure   arrival

À quelle heure part l'avion pour Lyon? *(kel) (uhr) (lee-oh⁽ⁿ⁾)* _____
at what time leaves for

À quelle heure part le train pour Londres? *(loh⁽ⁿ⁾-druh)* _____

À quelle heure arrive l'avion de New York? *(ah-reev)* _____
arrives from

À quelle heure arrive le train de Grenoble? *(gruh-noh-bluh)* _____

À quelle heure part l'avion pour Nice? *(nees)* _____

Vous have just arrived **en France. Vous êtes à la gare. Où voudriez-vous aller? À Limoges?** *(voo-dree-ay-voo)*
at   would you like

À Strasbourg? Tell that to the person at the **guichet** selling **les billets!** *(ghee-shay)*
window

Je voudrais aller en Bretagne. *(bruh-tahn-yuh)* _____
go

À quelle heure part le train pour la Bretagne? *(kel)* _____

Combien coûte le billet pour la Bretagne? *(koot)* _____

84

Maintenant that **vous** know the words essential for traveling **en France ou en Suisse**, what are some speciality items **vous** might go in search of?

(froh-mahzh)
le fromage
cheese

(soo-vuh-neer)
les souvenirs
souvenirs

(shoh-koh-laht)
des chocolates
chocolates

(vet-mah$^{(n)}$)
les vêtements
clothes

(par-fuh$^{(n)}$)
le parfum
perfume

(tah-bloh)
les tableaux
pictures

Your Pocket Pal™ can be found at the back of this book. Each section focuses on essentials for your **voyage**. Cut out your Pocket Pal™, fold it **et** carry it with you at all times. It does not matter whether **vous** carry it in your pocket, briefcase, knapsack **ou** wallet. Do not pack it in your luggage, as it will not be much help to you in your suitcase. Your Pocket Pal™ is not meant to replace learning **français**, but will help you in the event **vous** forget something and need a little bit of help.

□ **le zèbre** *(zeh-bruh)* . . . . zebra
   – **zébré** *(zay-bray)* . . . . striped
□ **le zèle** *(zel)* . . . . zeal, ardor   **Z**
   – **zélé** *(zay-lay)* . . . . zealous
□ **le zénith** *(zay-neet)* . . . . zenith, peak

20 La (kart) Carte ou Le (muh-new) Menu
menu

Vous êtes maintenant en France et vous avez une chambre. Vous avez (fa(n)) **faim. Où** (yah-teel) **y a-t-il**
have hunger is there

un bon restaurant? First of all, (eel-yah) **il y a** different types of places to eat. Let's learn them.
there are

(reh-stoh-rah(n))
le restaurant _____

exactly what it says with a variety of meals and prices

(brah-suh-ree)
la brasserie _____

originally a beer salon, but now also a restaurant

(loh-bairzh)
l'auberge _____

originally a country inn, but it can be an inviting city restaurant as well

(bee-stroh)
le bistro _____

slang for **le bar** or a small, intimate restaurant with lots of atmosphere

(bar)
le bar _____

serves morning pastries, but concentrates on liquid refreshments

If **vous** look around you **dans un restaurant français, vous** will see that some (koo-tewm) **coutumes**
customs

françaises might be different from yours. Sharing **tables avec** others **est** a common **et très**

pleasant custom. Before beginning **votre** (ruh-pah) **repas,** be sure to wish those sharing your table –
meal

(boh(n)) (nah-pay-tee)
"**Bon appétit!**" Your turn to practice now.
enjoy your meal

_____
(enjoy your meal)

And at least one more time for practice!

_____
(enjoy your meal)

❏ **le zéphyr** *(zay-feer)* . . . . balmy breeze _____
❏ **zéro** *(zay-roh)* . . . . zero _____
❏ **le zodiaque** *(zoh-dee-ahk)* . . . . zodiac **Z** _____
  – **Je suis Poissons.** *(zhuh)(swee)(pwah-soh(n))* . . I am a "pisces." _____
❏ **la zoologie** *(zoh-oh-loh-zhee)* . . . . zoology _____

Start imagining now all the new taste treats you will experience abroad. Try all of the different

types of eating establishments mentioned on the previous page. Experiment. If **vous trouvez un restaurant** that **vous voudriez** to try, consider calling ahead to make a **réservation.** *(ray-zair-vah-syoh⁽ⁿ⁾)*

<u>**"Je voudrais faire une réservation."**</u> If **vous avez besoin d'un menu**, catch the attention of **le**
I   would like

serveur, saying,

> **"Monsieur! Le menu, s'il vous plaît."**

––
(Sir! The menu, please.)

If your **serveur** asks if **vous** enjoyed your

repas, a smile **et** a **"Oui, merci,"** will tell him

that you did.

Most **restaurants français** post **le menu** outside **ou** inside. Do not hesitate to ask to see **la carte**

before being seated so **vous savez** what type of **repas et** **prix vous** will encounter. Most *(pree)*
                                                                meals   prices

restaurants offer **un plat du jour ou un menu à prix fixe.** These are complete **repas** at a fair
               daily special   fixed   meals

prix. Don't forget to take your Pocket Pal™ with you.
price

❒ **la zone** *(zohn)*	zone		_____
– une zone de silence *(see-lah⁽ⁿ⁾s)*	quiet zone		_____
❒ **le zoo** *(zoh)*	zoo	**Z**	_____
– un jardin zoologique *(zhar-da⁽ⁿ⁾)*	zoological garden		_____
❒ **Zut!** *(zewt)*	Darn! Rats!		_____

En France, *(eel-yah)* **il y a trois** main **repas** *(ruh-pah)* to enjoy every day, plus perhaps **un café et une pâtisserie** *(pah-tee-suh-ree)*
there are

pour le voyageur fatigué late in **l'après-midi.**

(puh-tee-day-zhuh-nay)
le **petit-déjeuner** _____
breakfast

    This meal usually consists of **café ou thé**, croissants, butter and marmalade.

    Check serving times before **vous** retire for the night or you might miss out!

(day-zhuh-nay)
le **déjeuner** _____
mid-day meal

    generally served from 12:00 to 14:00; you will be able to find any type

    of meal, **grand ou petit**, served at this time.

(dee-nay)
le **dîner** _____
evening meal

    generally served from 19:30 to 22:00. This meal is meant to be relished,

    surrounded by good friends and a pleasant atmosphere.

Maintenant for a preview of delights to come . . . At the back of this **livre, vous** will find a sample

menu français. *(lee-zay)* **Lisez le menu aujourd'hui et** *(ah-pruh-nay)* **apprenez les** *(noo-voh)* **nouveaux mots.** When **vous** are
read   today   learn

ready to leave on your **voyage,** cut out **le menu,** fold it, **et** carry it in your pocket, wallet **ou** purse.

Before you go, how do **vous** say these **trois** phrases which are so very important for the hungry

traveler?

Excuse me. I would like to make a reservation. _____

Waiter! The menu, please. _____

Enjoy your meal! _____

_____ *(mah⁽ⁿ⁾zh)* **mange des escargots?** _____ *(bwah)* **boit du thé?**
(who)   eats   (who)   drinks

(who)

_____ *(kay-bek)* **voyage à Québec?**
(who)

Learning the following should help you to identify what kind of meat **vous** have ordered **et comment** it will be prepared.

❏ **boeuf** *(buf)* . . . . beef   _____
❏ **veau** *(voh)* . . . . veal   _____
❏ **porc** *(por)* . . . . pork   _____
❏ **mouton** *(moo-toh⁽ⁿ⁾)* . . . . mutton   _____

La carte below has the main categories **vous** will find in most restaurants. Learn them **aujourd'hui** so that **vous** will easily recognize them when you dine **à Paris ou à Nice.** Be sure to write the words in the blanks below.

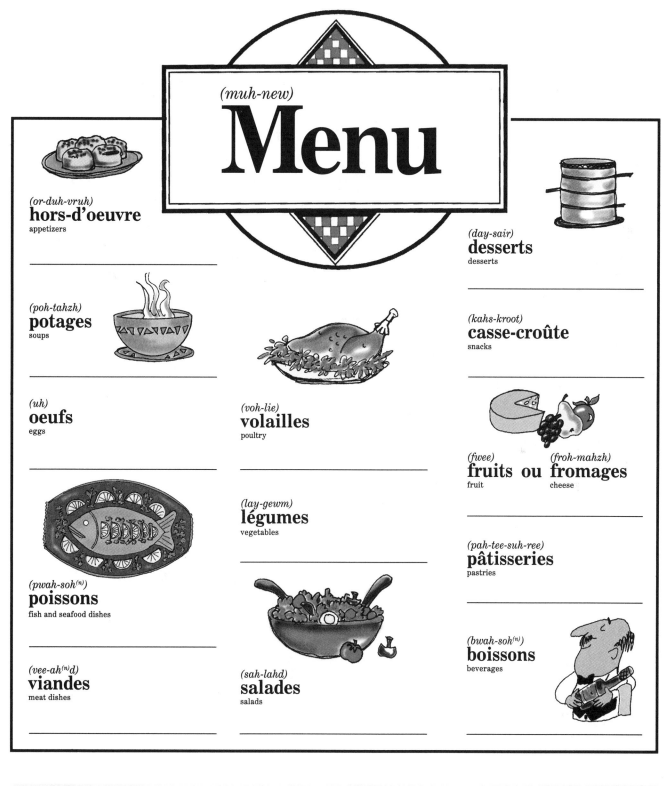

(muh-new)
Menu

(or-duh-vruh)
hors-d'oeuvre
appetizers

_____

(poh-tahzh)
potages
soups

_____

(uh)
oeufs
eggs

(pwah-soh$^{(n)}$)
poissons
fish and seafood dishes

_____

(vee-ah$^{(n)}$d)
viandes
meat dishes

(voh-lie)
volailles
poultry

_____

(lay-gewm)
légumes
vegetables

_____

(sah-lahd)
salades
salads

(day-sair)
desserts
desserts

_____

(kahs-kroot)
casse-croûte
snacks

_____

(fwee)   *(froh-mahzh)*
fruits ou fromages
fruit   cheese

_____

(pah-tee-suh-ree)
pâtisseries
pastries

_____

(bwah-soh$^{(n)}$)
boissons
beverages

☐ **volaille** *(voh-lie)*	poultry	_____
☐ **agneau** *(ahn-yoh)*	lamb	_____
☐ **gibier** *(zhee-bee-ay)*	game	_____
☐ **frit** *(free)*	fried	_____
☐ **rôti** *(roh-tee)*	roasted	_____

89

Vous may also order **légumes avec votre repas** *(lay-gewn)* *(ruh-pah)* **ou** perhaps **une salade verte** *(vairt)*. One day at an
vegetables   meal   green

open-air **marché** *(mar-shay)* will teach you **les noms** for all the different kinds of **légumes et fruits** *(fwee)*, plus it
market   fuit

will be a delightful experience for you. **Vous pouvez** always consult your menu guide at the back
can

of **ce** *(suh)* **livre** if **vous** *(voo)* **oubliez** *(zoo-blee-ay)* **le nom correct**. **Maintenant vous** are seated **et le serveur arrive** *(ah-reev)*.
this   forget   waiter

> **La carte, s'il vous plaît.**

> **Et comme boisson?**

> **Un verre de vin blanc, s'il vous plaît.**

Le petit-déjeuner *(puh-tee-day-zhuh-nay)* **est un peu** *(puh)* **différent** *(dee-fay-rah(n))* because **il est** fairly standardized **et vous** will
breakfast   little

frequently take it at **votre hôtel**, as **il est généralement** *(zhay-nay-rahl-mah(n))* included in **le prix de votre chambre**.
price   room

En bas il y a des exemples of what **vous pouvez** expect to greet you **le matin**.

Boissons   et . . .

café   pain

café au lait   croissants

thé   jambon
                                                ham

chocolat   confiture
                                                jam

jus d'orange   beurre
juice

jus de tomate   oeuf à la coque
                                                soft-boiled

jus de pomme   oeufs brouillés
apple   scrambled

lait   omelette nature

☐ **cuit** *(kwee)* . . . . cooked   _____
☐ **cuit au four** *(kwee)(toh)(foor)* . . . . baked   _____
☐ **grillé** *(gree-ay)* . . . . grilled   _____
☐ **farci** *(far-see)* . . . . stuffed   _____
☐ **fumé** *(few-may)* . . . . smoked   _____

Voilà an example of what **vous** might select for your evening meal. Using your menu guide on pages 117 and 118, as well as what **vous** have learned in this Step, fill in the blanks *in English* with what **vous** believe your **serveur** will bring you. **Les réponses sont** below.

Hors-d'oeuvre
Oeufs durs mayonnaise

_____

Salade
Salade niçoise avec du pain frais

_____

Entrée
Côtes d'agneau grillées à la menthe et au vinaigre

_____

Dessert
Mousse au chocolat

_____

(when)

(how)

(why)

LES RÉPONSES

Appetizer: Hard-boiled eggs with mayonnaise
Salad: Mixed salad with tuna, string beans and potatoes
Entree: Grilled lamb chops with mint sauce
Dessert: Chocolate mousse

Maintenant est a good time for a quick review. Draw lines between **les mots français et** their English equivalents.

we eat

waitress

give me

beverages

thank you

I would like

I drink

bill

tip

lunch

mail

breakfast

dinner

l'addition

le déjeuner

merci

le dîner

la serveuse

le petit-déjeuner

(bwah-soh⁽ⁿ⁾)
les **boissons**

donnez-moi

le courrier

(poor-bwahr)
le **pourboire**

je bois

nous mangeons

je voudrais

Voilà a few holidays which you might experience during your visit.
- ☐ **Nouvel An** *(noo-vel)(ah⁽ⁿ⁾)* . . . . New Year's Day
- ☐ **Noël** *(noh-el)* . . . . Christmas
- ☐ **Vendredi-Saint** *(vah⁽ⁿ⁾-druh-dee-sa⁽ⁿ⁾t)* . . . . Good Friday
- ☐ **Pâques** *(pah-kuh)* . . . . Easter

Qu'est-ce *(kess)* **qui est différent** *(key)* about **le téléphone en France?** Well, **vous** never notice such things
what
until **vous** want to use them. **Les téléphones** allow you to call **des amis,** *(day) (zah-mee)* reserve **les billets de**
friends   tickets
théâtre, de concert ou de ballet, *(bah-leh)* make emergency calls, check on the hours of a **musée,** *(mew-zay)* rent
une voiture et all those other **choses** which **nous faisons** on a daily basis. It also gives you a
do
certain amount of **liberté quand vous pouvez** make your own **appels de téléphone.** *(ah-pel)*
calls

Les téléphones can usually be found

everywhere: in the **bureaux de poste,** on the
post offices
street, in the **cafés,** at **la gare** and in the

lobby of **votre hôtel.**

So, let's learn how to operate **le téléphone.**

The instructions can look complicated,

but remember, **vous** should be able to

recognize some of these **mots** already. Most

téléphones use **une télécarte.** *(tay-lay-kart)* **Vous pouvez**
telephone card
buy **ces télécartes** *(say)* at news-stands and in
these
stores as well as **aux bureaux de poste et**

à la gare. Ready? Well, before you turn
train station
the page it would be a good idea to go back

et review all your numbers one more time.

To dial from the United States to most other countries **vous** need that country's international

area code. Your **annuaire** *(ah-new-air)* at home should have a listing of international area codes.
telephone book

Voilà some very useful words built around the word **"téléphone."** _____
☐ **le téléphoniste** *(tay-lay-foh-neest)* . . . . operator _____
☐ **le cabine téléphonique** *(kah-been)(tay-lay-foh-neek)* . . . . telephone booth _____
☐ **l'annuaire** *(lah-new-air)* . . . . telephone book _____
☐ **la conversation téléphonique** *(koh$^{(n)}$-vair-sah-syoh$^{(n)}$)* . . . . telephone conversation _____

When **vous** leave your contact numbers with friends, family **et** business colleagues, **vous** should

include your destination's country code **et** city code whenever possible . For example,

Country Codes		City Codes	
France	33	Paris	1
		Marseille	91
Belgium	32	Brussels	2
		Antwerp	3
Switzerland	41	Geneva	22

To call from one city to another **en France, vous** may need to go to **le bureau de poste ou** call

le téléphoniste dans votre hôtel. Tell **le téléphoniste**, "**Je voudrais téléphoner à Chicago**,"
_{operator}

ou "**Je voudrais téléphoner à San Francisco.**"

Now you try it: _____
(I would like to call . . .)

When answering **le téléphone, vous** pick up the receiver **et** say,

(ah-loh)   *(lah-pah-ray)*
"**Allô** c'est _____ **à l'appareil.**"
                    (votre nom)   on the phone

                                (ruh-vwahr)   *(duh-ma⁽ⁿ⁾)*
When saying goodbye, **vous dites**, "**Au revoir**," **ou** "**À demain.**" Your turn —
                                                    until tomorrow

_____
(Hello. This is . . .)

_____   _____
(goodbye)   (until tomorrow)

(noo-blee-ay)
N'oubliez pas that **vous pouvez** ask . . .
don't forget   can

(kohm-bya⁽ⁿ⁾) *(koot)*   *(ah-pel)*   *(oh)* *(zay-tah-zoo-nee)*
Combien coûte un appel téléphonique aux États-Unis? _____
                                                              U.S.A.

Combien coûte un appel téléphonique au Canada? _____

Voilà some emergency telephone numbers.
❑	**en France:**	**police** *(poh-lees)*	police	17	_____
		feu *(fuh)*	fire	18	_____
❑	**en Suisse:**	**police** *(poh-lees)*	police	117	_____
		feu *(fuh)*	fire	118	_____

Voilà some sample sentences for **le téléphone.** Write them in the blanks **en bas.**

(voo-dray) *(tay-lay-foh-nay)* *(boh-stoh[n])*
Je voudrais téléphoner à Boston. _____

(lah-ay-roh-por)
Je voudrais téléphoner à Air France à l'aéroport. _____

(oh) *(may-duh-sa[n])*
Je voudrais téléphoner au médecin. _____

(moh[n])
Mon numéro est 53-68-70-10. _____
my

(kel) *(ay)*
Quel est votre numéro de téléphone? _____
what

Quel est le numéro de téléphone de l'hôtel? _____

(lah-pah-ray)
Christine: **Allô, c'est Madame Villon à l'appareil. Je voudrais parler à Madame**

Beauchamp.

_____

(a[n]-stah[n]) *(may)* *(leen-yuh)*
Téléphoniste: **Un instant, s'il vous plaît. Excusez-moi, mais la ligne est occupée.**
one   but   line   busy

_____

(ray-pay-tay) *(plew)* *(lah[n]-tuh-mah[n])*
Christine: **Répétez ça, s'il vous plaît. Parlez plus lentement.**
speak   more   slowly

_____

Téléphoniste: **Excusez-moi, mais la ligne est occupée.**

_____

(oh) *(ruh-vwahr)*
Christine: **Oh. Merci. Au revoir.**

_____

Vous êtes ready to use any **téléphone en France.** Just take it **lentement** *(lah[n]-tuh-mah[n])* et speak clearly.
slowly

Voilà countries **vous** may wish to call.
- ☐ **Algérie** *(ahl-zhay-ree)* .... Algeria _____
- ☐ **Autriche** *(oh-treesh)* .... Austria _____
- ☐ **Belgique** *(bel-zheek)* .... Belgium _____
- ☐ **Canada** *(kah-nah-dah)* .... Canada _____

95

22

Le Métro
(may-troh)
subway

An excellent means of transportation **est le métro.** *(may-troh)* **Le métro à Paris est** the quickest **et**

cheapest form of **transport.** *(trah⁽ⁿ⁾-spor)* transportation **Le métro est** an extensive **système** *(see-stem)* which has been expanded by

an express line to the suburbs, **le RER.** **Il y a toujours l'autobus** *(air-uh-air)* *(too-zhoor)* there is always which is a slower but more

scenic form of **transport.** *(trah⁽ⁿ⁾-spor)*

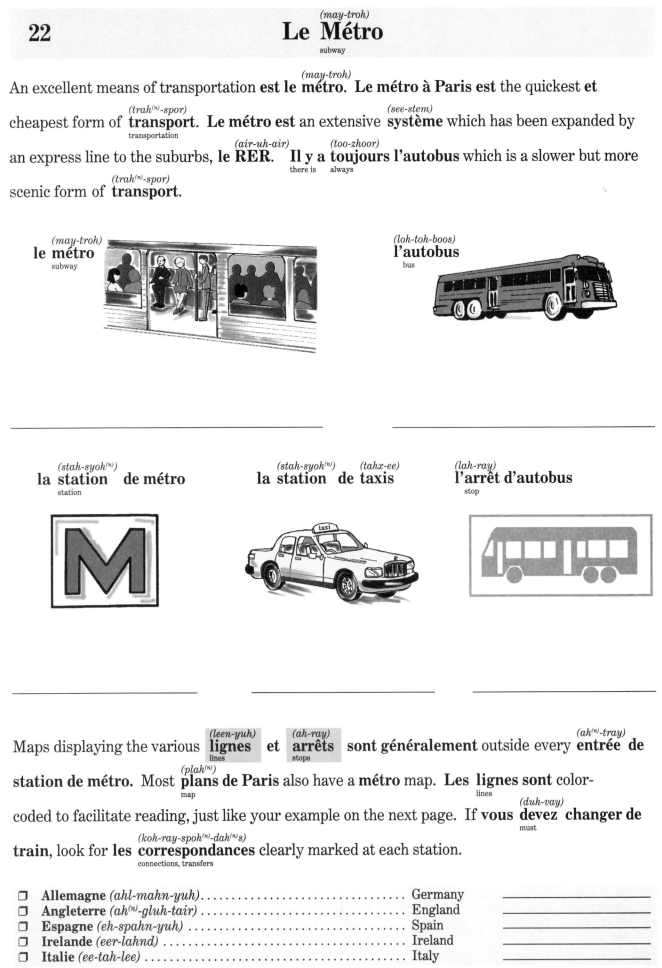

le métro *(may-troh)*
subway

l'autobus *(loh-toh-boos)*
bus

la station de métro *(stah-syoh⁽ⁿ⁾)*
station

la station de taxis *(stah-syoh⁽ⁿ⁾)* *(tahx-ee)*

l'arrêt d'autobus *(lah-ray)*
stop

Maps displaying the various **lignes** *(leen-yuh)* lines **et arrêts** *(ah-ray)* stops **sont généralement** outside every **entrée de** *(ah⁽ⁿ⁾-tray)*

station de métro. Most **plans de Paris** *(plah⁽ⁿ⁾)* map also have a **métro** map. **Les lignes sont** lines color-

coded to facilitate reading, just like your example on the next page. If **vous devez changer de** *(duh-vay)* must

train, look for **les correspondances** *(koh-ray-spoh⁽ⁿ⁾-dah⁽ⁿ⁾s)* connections, transfers clearly marked at each station.

❏ **Allemagne** *(ahl-mahn-yuh)*...........................	Germany	_____
❏ **Angleterre** *(ah⁽ⁿ⁾-gluh-tair)*........................	England	_____
❏ **Espagne** *(eh-spahn-yuh)*.............................	Spain	_____
❏ **Irelande** *(eer-lahnd)*.................................	Ireland	_____
❏ **Italie** *(ee-tah-lee)*....................................	Italy	_____

Other than having foreign words, **le métro français** functions just like **à Londres ou à New York**. Locate your destination, select the correct line on your practice **métro et** hop on board.

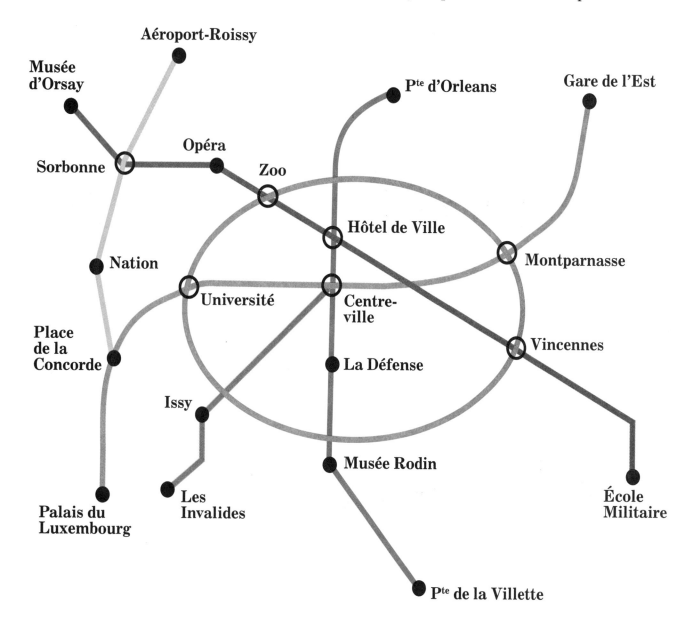

Say these questions aloud many times and don't forget you need **un billet pour le métro!**

Où est la station de métro?
(stah-syoh⁽ⁿ⁾) *(may-troh)*

Où est la station de taxis?

Où est l'arrêt d'autobus?

☐ **Luxembourg** *(lewk-sah⁽ⁿ⁾-boor)*............ Luxembourg
☐ **les Pays-Bas** *(lay)(pay-ee-bah)*............ Netherlands
☐ **Afrique du Sud** *(ah-freek)(dew)(sood)*...... South Africa
☐ **Suisse** *(swees)*................. Switzerland
☐ **les États-Unis** *(lay)(zay-tah-zoo-nee)*...... the United States

Practice the following basic questions out loud **et** then write them in the blanks below.

1. *(kel)* **Quelle** est la **fréquence** *(fray-kah⁽ⁿ⁾s)* des trains pour le Louvre? _____
   what   is   frequency/how often   *(day)*

   Quelle est la **fréquence des autobus pour Montparnasse?** _____

   Quelle est la **fréquence des trains pour l'aéroport?** *(lah-ay-roh-por)* _____

2. *(kah⁽ⁿ⁾)* **Quand le train part-il?** *(par-teel)* _____
   when   does it leave

   Quand l'autobus part-il? _____ Quand l'autobus part-il? _____

3. *(koot)* *(tee-kay)* **Combien coûte un ticket de métro?** _____

   Combien coûte un ticket d'autobus? _____

   (tah-reef)(say) **Le tarif, c'est combien?** _____
   fare   it is   how much

   Le ticket, c'est combien? _____

4. *(oo)* *(stah-syoh⁽ⁿ⁾)* **Où est la station de métro?** _____

   Où est la station de taxis? _____

   (lah-ray) **Où est l'arrêt d'autobus?** _____

Let's change directions **et** learn **trois** new verbs. **Vous** know the basic "plug-in" formula, so

write out your own sentences using these new verbs.

(lah-vay) **laver** _____
to wash (clothes)

(pair-druh) **perdre** _____
to lose

(eel)(foh) **il faut** _____
it is necessary (it takes)

Voilà a few more holidays to keep in mind.
- ☐ **Fête du Travail** *(fet)(dew)(trah-vy)* . . . . Labor Day
- ☐ **Fête Nationale** *(fet)(nah-syoh-nahl)* . . . . National/Bastille Day
- ☐ **Armistice** *(ar-mees-tees)* . . . . Victory Day 1945
- ☐ **Toussaint** *(too-sa⁽ⁿ⁾t)* . . . . All Saints' Day (Nov. 1)

La Vente et l'Achat
(vah⁽ⁿ⁾t) selling   *(lah-shah)* buying

Shopping abroad is exciting. The simple everyday task of buying **un litre** *(lee-truh)* liter **de lait** *(lay)* milk **ou une pomme** *(pohm)* apple becomes a challenge that **vous** should **maintenant** be able to meet quickly **et** easily. Of course, **vous** will purchase **des souvenirs** *(soo-vuh-neer)* souvenirs**, des timbres-poste et des cartes postales** but do not forget those many other items ranging from shoelaces to **aspirine** *(ah-spee-reen)* aspirin that **vous** might need unexpectedly. Locate your store, draw a line to it **et**, as always, write your new words in the blanks provided.

le grand magasin *(grah⁽ⁿ⁾) (mah-gah-za⁽ⁿ⁾)* _____
department store

le cinéma *(see-nay-mah)* _____
cinema

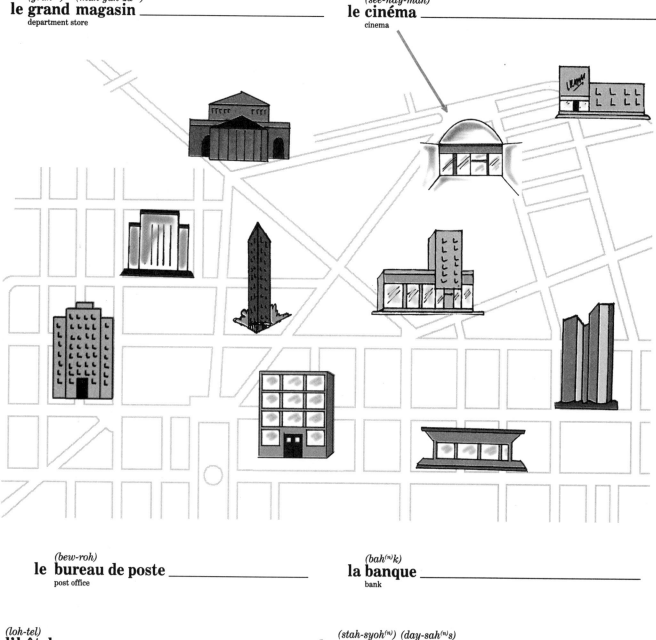

le bureau de poste *(bew-roh)* _____
post office

la banque *(bah⁽ⁿ⁾k)* _____
bank

l'hôtel *(loh-tel)* _____
hotel

la station d'essence *(stah-syoh⁽ⁿ⁾) (day-sah⁽ⁿ⁾s)* _____
service station

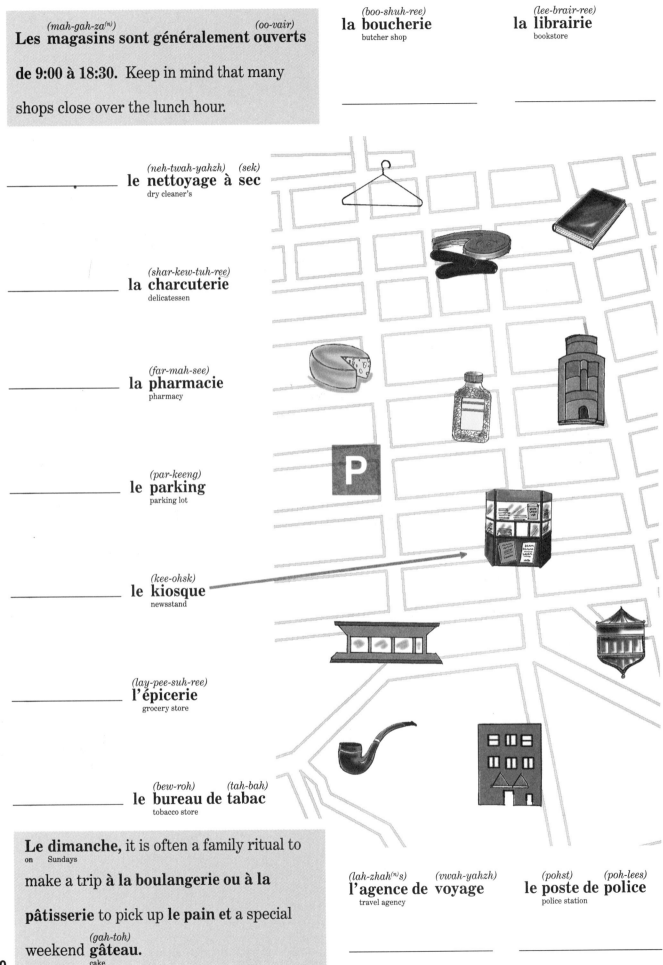

Les **magasins** sont généralement **ouverts**
(mah-gah-za⁽ⁿ⁾) *(oo-vair)*
de 9:00 à 18:30. Keep in mind that many
shops close over the lunch hour.

la **boucherie**
(boo-shuh-ree)
butcher shop

la **librairie**
(lee-brair-ree)
bookstore

_____ le **nettoyage à sec**
(neh-twah-yahzh) *(sek)*
dry cleaner's

_____ la **charcuterie**
(shar-kew-tuh-ree)
delicatessen

_____ la **pharmacie**
(far-mah-see)
pharmacy

_____ le **parking**
(par-keeng)
parking lot

_____ le **kiosque**
(kee-ohsk)
newsstand

_____ l'**épicerie**
(lay-pee-suh-ree)
grocery store

_____ le **bureau de tabac**
(bew-roh) *(tah-bah)*
tobacco store

Le dimanche, it is often a family ritual to
on   Sundays

make a trip **à la boulangerie ou à la**

pâtisserie to pick up **le pain et** a special

weekend **gâteau.**
(gah-toh)
cake

l'**agence de voyage**
(lah-zhah⁽ⁿ⁾s) *(vwah-yahzh)*
travel agency

le **poste de police**
(pohst) *(poh-lees)*
police station

100

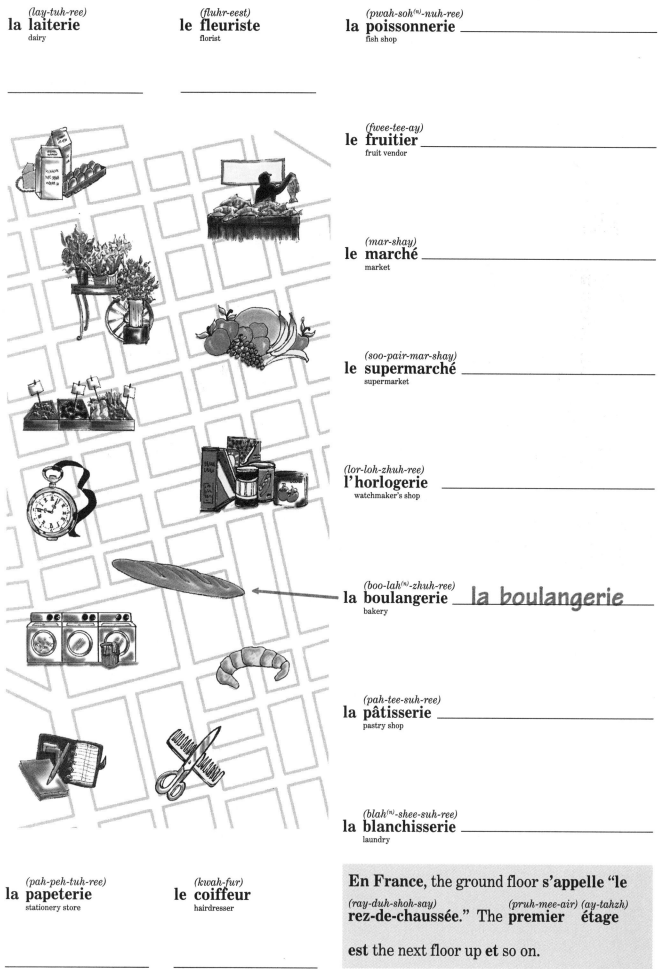

(lay-tuh-ree)
la laiterie
dairy

_____

(fluhr-eest)
le fleuriste
florist

_____

(pwah-soh⁽ⁿ⁾-nuh-ree)
la poissonnerie _____
fish shop

(fwee-tee-ay)
le fruitier _____
fruit vendor

(mar-shay)
le marché _____
market

(soo-pair-mar-shay)
le supermarché _____
supermarket

(lor-loh-zhuh-ree)
l'horlogerie _____
watchmaker's shop

(boo-lah⁽ⁿ⁾-zhuh-ree)
la boulangerie *la boulangerie* _____
bakery

(pah-tee-suh-ree)
la pâtisserie _____
pastry shop

(blah⁽ⁿ⁾-shee-suh-ree)
la blanchisserie _____
laundry

(pah-peh-tuh-ree)
la papeterie
stationery store

_____

(kwah-fur)
le coiffeur
hairdresser

_____

En France, the ground floor **s'appelle** "le
(ray-duh-shoh-say) *(pruh-mee-air) (ay-tahzh)*
rez-de-chaussée." The **premier étage**

est the next floor up **et** so on.

24   Le Grand Magasin
(grah⁽ⁿ⁾) *(mah-gah-za⁽ⁿ⁾)*
department store

At this point, **vous** should just about be ready for **votre voyage**. **Vous** have gone shopping for those last-minute odds 'n ends. Most likely, the store directory at your local **grand magasin** did not look like the one **en bas**! **Vous savez** that "**enfant**" is French for "<u>child</u>" so if **vous avez besoin de** something for a child, **vous** would probably look on the **deuxième ou troisième étage, n'est-ce pas**?

4ᴹᴱ ÉTAGE	vaisselle cristal lampes tapis	service de table ameublement de cuisine lits	clés faïence porcelaine miroirs
3ᴹᴱ ÉTAGE	disques télévisions meubles d'enfant jouets	radios instruments de musique papeterie	tabac restaurant journaux revues
2ᴹᴱ ÉTAGE	tout pour l'enfant vêtements de femme chapeaux de femme	vêtements d'homme chaussures d'enfant photo livres	toilettes antiquités ameublement tableaux

1ᴱᴿ ÉTAGE	accessoires d'auto
	lingerie
	mouchoirs
	maillots de bain
		chaussures de
		  femme
		chaussures d'homme
			équipement de
			  sport
			outils
			mobilier de camping

R	parapluies cartes chapeaux d'homme bijouterie	gants maroquinerie chaussettes ceintures	pendules/montres parfumerie confiserie caféteria

Let's start a checklist **pour votre voyage**. Besides **vêtements, de quoi avez-vous besoin?** As you learn these **mots,** assemble these items **dans un coin** of your **maison**. Check **et** make sure that they **sont propres et** ready **pour votre voyage**. Be sure to do the same **avec le reste des choses** that **vous** pack. On the next pages, match each item to its picture, draw a line to it and write out the word many times. As **vous** organize these things, check them off on this list. Do not forget to take the next group of sticky labels and label these **choses aujourd'hui.**

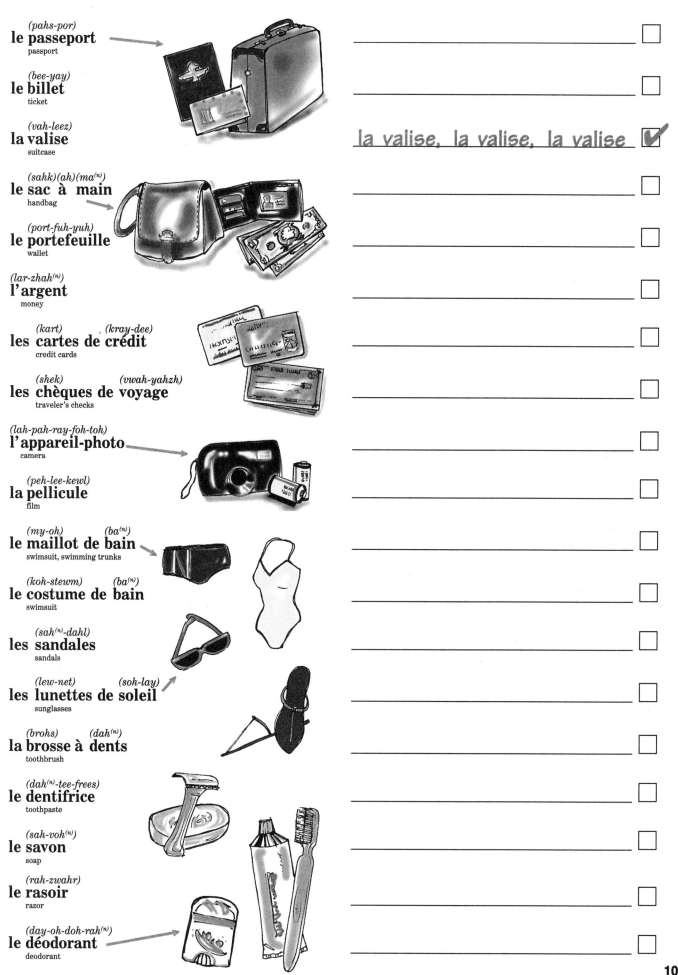

(pahs-por)
le passeport
passport

_____ ☐

(bee-yay)
le billet
ticket

_____ ☐

(vah-leez)
la valise
suitcase

la valise, la valise, la valise ☑

(sahk)(ah)(ma^{(n)})
le sac à main
handbag

_____ ☐

(port-fuh-yuh)
le portefeuille
wallet

_____ ☐

(lar-zhah^{(n)})
l'argent
money

_____ ☐

(kart) *(kray-dee)*
les cartes de crédit
credit cards

_____ ☐

(shek) *(vwah-yahzh)*
les chèques de voyage
traveler's checks

_____ ☐

(lah-pah-ray-foh-toh)
l'appareil-photo
camera

_____ ☐

(peh-lee-kewl)
la pellicule
film

_____ ☐

(my-oh) *(ba^{(n)})*
le maillot de bain
swimsuit, swimming trunks

_____ ☐

(koh-stewm) *(ba^{(n)})*
le costume de bain
swimsuit

_____ ☐

(sah^{(n)}-dahl)
les sandales
sandals

_____ ☐

(lew-net) *(soh-lay)*
les lunettes de soleil
sunglasses

_____ ☐

(brohs) *(dah^{(n)})*
la brosse à dents
toothbrush

_____ ☐

(dah^{(n)}-tee-frees)
le dentifrice
toothpaste

_____ ☐

(sah-voh^{(n)})
le savon
soap

_____ ☐

(rah-zwahr)
le rasoir
razor

_____ ☐

(day-oh-doh-rah^{(n)})
le déodorant
deodorant

_____ ☐

(pen-yuh)
le peigne
comb

le peigne, le peigne ✔

(mah(n)-toh)
le manteau
raincoat

(pah-rah-plew-ee)
le parapluie
umbrella

(la(n)-pair-may-ah-bluh)
l'imperméable
overcoat

(gah(n))
les gants
gloves

(shah-poh)
le chapeau
hat

(shah-poh)
le chapeau
hat

(boht)
les bottes
boots

(shoh-suhr)
les chaussures
shoes

(shoh-suhr) (teh-nees)
les chaussures de tennis
tennis shoes

(koh(n)-play)
le complet
suit

(krah-vaht)
la cravate
tie

(shuh-meez)
la chemise
shirt

(moo-shwahr)
le mouchoir
handkerchief

(veh-stoh(n))
le veston
jacket, blazer

(pah(n)-tah-loh(n))
le pantalon
trousers

(jeans)
les jeans
jeans

(short)
le short
shorts

(tee-shirt)
le teeshirt
T-shirt

(sleep)
le slip
underpants
☐

(tree-koh) **(poh)**
le tricot de peau →
undershirt
☐

(rohb)
la robe
dress
☐

(blooz)
la blouse
blouse
☐

(zhewp)
la jupe
skirt
la jupe, la jupe, la jupe ✔

(shah⁽ⁿ⁾-dye)
le chandail →
sweater
☐

(koh⁽ⁿ⁾-bee-nay-zoh⁽ⁿ⁾)
la combinaison
slip
☐

(soo-tya⁽ⁿ⁾-gorzh)
le soutien-gorge
brassiere
☐

(sleep)
le slip
underpants
☐

(shoh-set)
les chaussettes
socks
☐

(bah)
les bas
pantyhose
☐

(pee-zhah-mah)
le pyjama
pajamas
☐

(shuh-meez) **(nwee)**
la chemise de nuit
nightshirt
☐

(rohb) **(shah⁽ⁿ⁾-bruh)**
la robe de chambre
bathrobe
☐

(pah⁽ⁿ⁾-too-fluh)
les pantoufles
slippers
☐

(sah-voh⁽ⁿ⁾)
From now on, **vous avez** "savon" **et non pas** "soap." Having assembled these **choses, vous**
you have things
(shohz)

are ready **voyager.** Let's add these important shopping phrases to your basic repetoire.
to travel

(kel) **(tie)**
Quelle taille? _____
what size

(sah) (muh) (vah)
Ça me va. _____
it fits me

(nuh)(muh)(vah) (pah)
Ça ne me va pas. _____
it does not fit me

105

Treat yourself to a final review. **Vous savez** *(sah-vay)* know **les noms pour les magasins français**, so let's practice shopping. Just remember your key question **mots** that you learned in Step 2. Whether **vous** need to buy **un chapeau** *(shah-poh)* **ou un livre** the necessary **mots** are the same.

1.   First step — **où?**

Où est la laiterie? *(lay-tuh-ree)*   **Où est la banque?** *(bah⁽ⁿ⁾k)*   **Où est le kiosque?** *(kee-ohsk)*

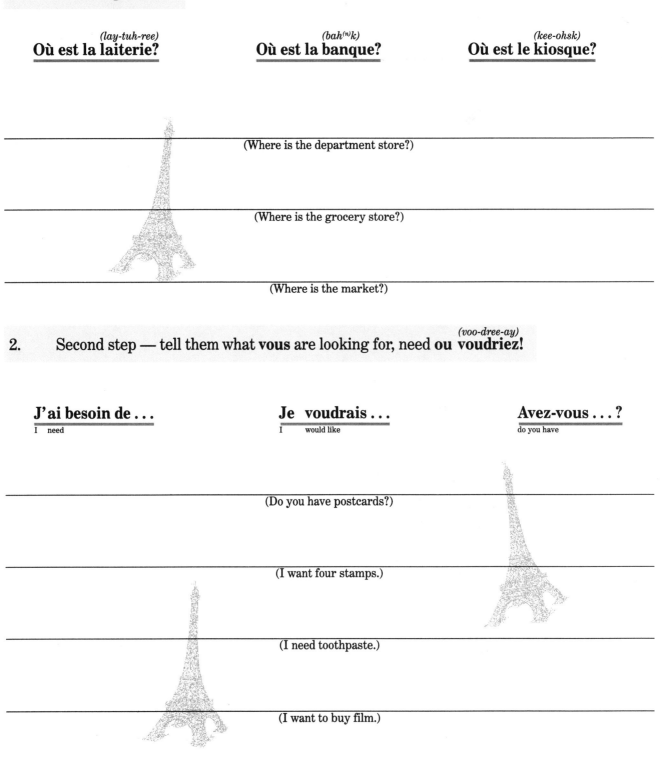

_____ (Where is the department store?)

_____ (Where is the grocery store?)

_____ (Where is the market?)

2.   Second step — tell them what **vous** are looking for, need **ou voudriez!** *(voo-dree-ay)*

J'ai besoin de . . .   **Je voudrais . . .**   **Avez-vous . . . ?**
I   need   I   would like   do you have

_____ (Do you have postcards?)

_____ (I want four stamps.)

_____ (I need toothpaste.)

_____ (I want to buy film.)

_____ (Do you have coffee?)

Go through the glossary at the end of this **livre et** select **vingt mots.** Drill the above patterns

avec ces vingt mots. Don't cheat. Drill them **aujourd'hui.** **Maintenant,** take **encore vingt**
  (say) / these · *(ah(n)-kor)* / more

mots de votre glossary **et** do the same.

3.   Third step — find out **combien ça coûte.**
                          (kohm-bya(n)) (sah) (koot)

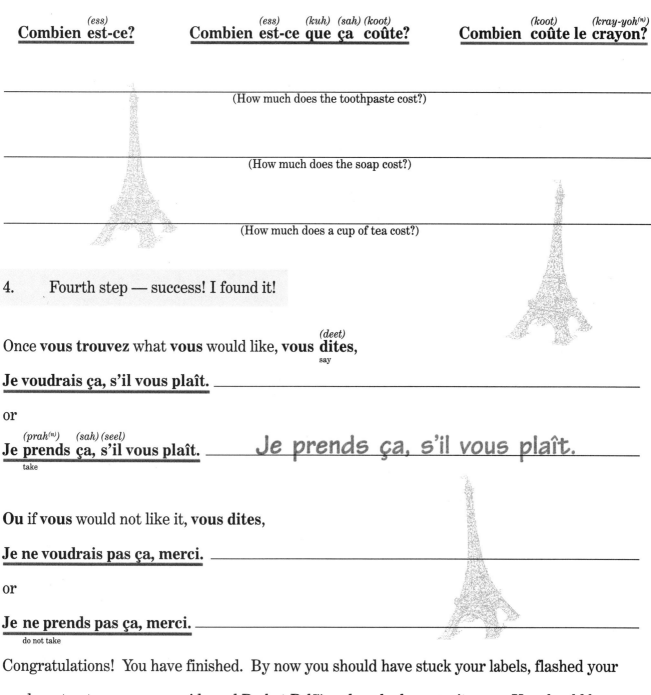

Combien est-ce?   **Combien est-ce que ça coûte?**   **Combien coûte le crayon?**
   (ess)   *(ess)   (kuh) (sah) (koot)*   *(koot)   (kray-yoh(n))*

_____

(How much does the toothpaste cost?)

_____

(How much does the soap cost?)

_____

(How much does a cup of tea cost?)

4.   Fourth step — success! I found it!

Once **vous trouvez** what **vous** would like, **vous dites,**
                                               (deet) / say

Je voudrais ça, s'il vous plaît. _____

or

Je prends ça, s'il vous plaît. ___ *Je prends ça, s'il vous plaît.* ___
   (prah(n)) (sah) (seel)
   take

Ou if **vous** would not like it, **vous dites,**

Je ne voudrais pas ça, merci. _____

or

Je ne prends pas ça, merci. _____
   do not take

Congratulations! You have finished. By now you should have stuck your labels, flashed your

cards, cut out your menu guide and Pocket Pal™ and packed your suitcases. You should be very

pleased with your accomplishment. You have learned what it sometimes takes others years to

achieve and you hopefully had fun doing it. **Bon voyage!**
                                          (boh(n))

Glossary

A

à *(ah)* . . . . at, to, in
à côté de *(ah)(koh-tay)(duh)* . . . . next to
à la française *(ah)(lah)(frah$^{(n)}$-sez)* . . in the French manner
accepter *(ahk-sep-tay)* . . . . to accept
accident, le *(ahk-see-dah$^{(n)}$)* . . . . accident
achat, le *(ah-shah)* . . . . purchase
acheter *(ah-shuh-tay)* . . . . to buy
addition, la *(ah-dee-syoh$^{(n)}$)* . . . . bill in a restaurant
admission, la *(ahd-mee-syoh$^{(n)}$)* . . . . admission
adresse, la *(ah-dress)* . . . . address
aéroport, le *(ah-ay-roh-por)* . . . . airport
Afrique, la *(ah-freek)* . . . . Africa
Afrique du Sud, la *(ah-freek)(dew)(sood)* . . . . . South Africa
agence de location des voitures, la *(ah-zhah$^{(n)}$s)(duh)(loh-kah-syoh$^{(n)}$)(duh)(vwah-tewr)* . . . . car-rental agency
agence de voyage, la *(ah-zhah$^{(n)}$s)(duh)(vwah-yahzh)* . . . . . .
. . . . travel agency
agneau, le *(ahn-yoh)* . . . . lamb
aidez-moi *(ay-day-mwah)* . . . . help me! aid me!
alcool, le *(ahl-kohl)* . . . . alcohol
Algérie, la *(ahl-zhay-ree)* . . . . Algeria
Allemagne, la *(ahl-mahn-yuh)* . . . . Germany
allemand (e) *(ahl-mah$^{(n)}$)* . . . . German
aller *(ah-lay)* . . . . to go, one way (ticket)
aller et retour *(ah-lay)(ay)(ruh-toor)* . . . . round trip
allô *(ah-loh)* . . . . hello (on telephone)
Alpes, les *(ahlp)* . . . . the Alps
alphabet, le *(ahl-fah-bay)* . . . . alphabet
américain (e) *(ah-may-ree-ka$^{(n)}$)* . . . . American
Amérique, la *(ah-may-reek)* . . . . America
amusez-vous *(ah-mew-zay-voo)* . . . . enjoy yourself!
an, le *(ah$^{(n)}$)* . . . . year
ancien (ancienne) *(ah$^{(n)}$-syah$^{(n)}$)* . . . . old
anglais (e) *(ah$^{(n)}$-glay)* . . . . English
Angleterre, la *(ah$^{(n)}$-gluh-tair)* . . . . England
animal, le *(ah-nee-mahl)* . . . . animal
année, la *(ah-nay)* . . . . year
annuaire, le *(ah-new-air)* . . . . telephone book
août, le *(oot)* . . . . August
appareil, le *(ah-pah-ray)* . . . . gadget, appliance
appareil-photo, le *(ah-pah-ray-foh-toh)* . . . . camera
appartement, le *(ah-par-teh-mah$^{(n)}$)* . . . . apartment
appel, le *(ah-pel)* . . . . call
appel téléphonique, le *(ah-pel)(tay-lay-foh-neek)* . . telephone call
s'appeler *(sah-puh-lay)* . . . . to be called
Comment vous appelez-vous? *(koh-moh$^{(n)}$)(voo)(zah-puh-lay-voo)* . . . . What is your name?
je m'appelle *(zhuh)(mah-pel)* . . . . my name is
appétit, le *(ah-pay-tee)* . . . . appetite
apprendre *(ah-prah$^{(n)}$-druh)* . . . . to learn
après-midi, le *(ah-preh-mee-dee)* . . . . afternoon
argent, le *(ar-zhah$^{(n)}$)* . . . . money
armoire, la *(ar-mwahr)* . . . . closet, wardrobe

arrêt, le *(ah-ray)* . . . . stop, arrest
arrivée, la *(ah-ree-vay)* . . . . arrival
arriver *(ah-ree-vay)* . . . . to arrive
aspirine, la *(ah-spee-reen)* . . . . aspirin
assiette, la *(ah-syet)* . . . . plate
assis (e) *(ah-see)* . . . . seated
attendre *(ah-tah$^{(n)}$-druh)* . . . . to wait for
attention, la *(ah-tah$^{(n)}$-syoh$^{(n)}$)* . . . . attention
au *(oh)* . . . . in, in the, at the
au-dessus de *(oh-duh-syoo)(duh)* . . . . over
au revoir *(oh)(ruh-vwahr)* . . . . goodbye
auberge, la *(oh-bairzh)* . . . . country inn
aujourd'hui *(oh-zhoor-dwee)* . . . . today
aussi *(oh-see)* . . . . also
auteur, le *(oh-tur)* . . . . author
auto, la *(oh-toh)* . . . . car
autobus, le *(oh-toh-boos)* . . . . bus
automne, le *(oh-tohn)* . . . . autumn
autorail, le *(oh-toh-rye)* . . . . slow train
autoroute, la *(oh-toh-root)* . . . . freeway
Autriche, la *(oh-treesh)* . . . . Austria
avec *(ah-vek)* . . . . with
avez *(ah-vay)* . . . . (you) have
avion, le *(ah-vyoh$^{(n)}$)* . . . . airplane
avoir *(ah-vwahr)* . . . . to have
j'ai *(zhay)* . . . . I have
nous avons *(noo)(zah-voh$^{(n)}$)* . . . . we have
avoir besoin de *(ah-vwahr)(buh-zwa$^{(n)}$)(duh)* . . . . . . to need
avril *(ah-vreel)* . . . . April

B

balcon, le *(bahl-koh$^{(n)}$)* . . . . balcony
ballet, le *(bah-leh)* . . . . ballet
ballon, le *(bah-loh$^{(n)}$)* . . . . balloon, big ball
banane, la *(bah-nahn)* . . . . banana
banc, le *(bah$^{(n)}$)* . . . . bench
banque, la *(bah$^{(n)}$k)* . . . . bank
bar, le *(bar)* . . . . type of café/restaurant
bas *(bah)* . . . . low
en bas *(ah$^{(n)}$)(bah)* . . . . below, downstairs
bas, les *(bah)* . . . . pantyhose
bateau, le *(bah-toh)* . . . . boat
beau *(boh)* . . . . beautiful
beaucoup *(boh-koo)* . . . . many, a lot
Belgique, la *(bel-zheek)* . . . . Belgium
belle *(bel)* . . . . beautiful
besoin, le *(buh-zwa$^{(n)}$)* . . . . need
beurre, le *(buhr)* . . . . butter
bicyclette, la *(bee-see-klet)* . . . . bicycle
bien *(bya$^{(n)}$)* . . . . well
pas bien *(pah)(bya$^{(n)}$)* . . . . not too well
bien sûr *(bya$^{(n)}$)(sur)* . . . . of course
bière, la *(bee-air)* . . . . beer
bifteck, le *(beef-tek)* . . . . beefsteak
billet, le *(bee-ay)* . . . . bank note, ticket

biscuit, le *(bee-skwee)* .... cookie
bistro, le *(bee-stroh)* .... café, restaurant
blanc (blanche) *(blah$^{(n)}$)* .... white
blanchisserie, la *(blah$^{(n)}$-shee-suh-ree)* .. laundromat, laundry
bleu (e) *(bluh)* .... blue
blouse, la *(blooz)* .... blouse
boeuf, le *(buf)* .... beef
boire *(bwahr)* .... to drink
boisson, la *(bwah-soh$^{(n)}$)* .... beverage
boîte aux lettres, la *(bwaht)(oh)(let-ruh)* .... mailbox
bon *(boh$^{(n)}$)* .... good
  bon appétit *(boh$^{(n)}$)(nah-pay-tee)* .... enjoy your meal
  bon marché *(boh$^{(n)}$)(mar-shay)* .... inexpensive
bonjour *(boh$^{(n)}$)(zhoor)* .... good morning, good day
bonne *(bun)* .... good
  bonne chance *(bun)(shah$^{(n)}$s)* .... good luck
  bonne nuit *(bun)(nwee)* .... good night
bonsoir *(boh$^{(n)}$-swahr)* .... good evening
botte, la *(boht)* .... boot
boucherie, la *(boo-shuh-ree)* .... butcher shop
boulangerie, la *(boo-lah$^{(n)}$-zhuh-ree)* .... bakery
bouteille, la *(boo-tay)* .... bottle
brasserie, la *(brah-suh-ree)* .... restaurant
bref (brève) *(brehf)* .... brief, short
brilliant (e) *(bree-yah$^{(n)}$)* ...... brilliant, sparkling
brosse à dents, la *(brohs)(ah)(dah$^{(n)}$)* .... toothbrush
brouillard, le *(broo-ee-yar)* .... fog
bureau, le *(bew-roh)* .... desk, office
bureau de change, le *(bew-roh)(duh)(shah$^{(n)}$zh)* ....
  .... money-exchange counter
bureau de poste, le *(bew-roh)(duh)(pohst)* ...... post office
bureau de tabac, le *(bew-roh)(duh)(tah-bah)* .. tobacco store
bureau des objets trouvés, le *(bew-roh)(day)(zohb-zhay)*
  (troo-vay) .... lost-and-found office

C

c'est *(say)* .... it is
c'était *(say-tay)* .... it was
ça *(sah)* .... that, it
  ça me va *(sah)(muh)(vah)* .... it fits me
cabine téléphonique, la *(kah-been)(tay-lay-foh-neek)* .....
  .... telephone booth
cabinets, les *(kah-bee-nay)* .... toilets
café, le *(kah-fay)* .... coffee, café
caisse, la *(kess)* .... cashier, register
calendrier, le *(kah-lah$^{(n)}$-dree-ay)* .... calendar
Canada, le *(kah-nah-dah)* .... Canada
canadien (canadienne) *(kah-nah-dya$^{(n)}$)* .... Canadian
canapé, le *(kah-nah-pay)* .... sofa
capitale, la *(kah-pee-tahl)* .... capital
carafe, la *(kah-rahf)* .... carafe
carte, la *(kart)* .... menu, map
carte de crédit, la *(kart)(duh)(kray-dee)* .... credit card
carte postale, la *(kart)(poh-stahl)* .... postcard
casse-croûte, le *(kahs-kroot)* .... snack
cathédrale, la *(kah-tay-drahl)* .... cathedral
catholique *(kah-toh-leek)* .... Catholic
ce, cette *(suh)*, *(set)* .... that, this
Celsius *(sel-see-ews)* .... Centigrade
cendrier, le *(sah$^{(n)}$-dree-ay)* .... ashtray
cent *(sah$^{(n)}$)* .... one hundred
centime, le *(sah$^{(n)}$-teem)* .... centime (part of a franc)
centre, le *(sah$^{(n)}$-truh)* .... center
ces *(say)* .... these, those
chaise, la *(shehz)* .... chair
chambre, la *(shah$^{(n)}$-bruh)* .... room
chambre à coucher, la *(shah$^{(n)}$-bruh)(ah)(koo-shay)* .. bedroom

champagne, le *(shah$^{(n)}$-pahn-yuh)* .... champagne
chandail, le *(shah$^{(n)}$-dye)* .... sweater
changement, le *(shah$^{(n)}$-zhuh-mah$^{(n)}$)* .... change
changer (de train, d'autobus) *(shah$^{(n)}$-zhay)* ....
  .... to transfer, change (train, bus)
chapeau, le *(shah-poh)* .... hat
charcuterie, la *(shar-kew-tuh-ree)* .... delicatessen
chat, le *(shah)* .... cat
château, le *(shah-toh)* .... castle
chaud (e) *(shoh)* .... hot
chaussette, la *(shoh-set)* .... sock
chaussure, la *(shoh-suhr)* .... shoe
chaussure de tennis, la *(shoh-suhr)(duh)(teh-nees)* ....
  .... tennis shoe
chemise, la *(shuh-meez)* .... shirt
chemise de nuit, la *(shuh-meez)(duh)(nwee)* .... nightshirt
chèque, le *(shek)* .... bank check
chèque de voyage, le *(shek)(duh)(vwah-yahzh)* ....
  .... traveler's check
cher (chère) *(shair)* .... expensive
chien, le *(shya$^{(n)}$)* .... dog
Chine, la *(sheen)* .... China
chocolat, le *(shoh-koh-lah)* .... chocolate
chose, la *(shohz)* .... thing
cinéma, le *(see-nay-mah)* .... cinema
cinq *(sank)* .... five
cinquante *(sang-kah$^{(n)}$t)* .... fifty
coiffeur, le *(kwah-fur)* .... hairdresser
coin, le *(kwa$^{(n)}$)* .... corner
combien *(kohm-bya$^{(n)}$)* .... how much
  Combien est-ce? *(kohm-bya$^{(n)}$)(ess)* ...... How much is it?
combinaison, la *(koh$^{(n)}$-bee-nay-zoh$^{(n)}$)* ... slip (undergarment)
commander *(koh-mah$^{(n)}$-day)* .... to order
comme *(kohm)* .... as
commencer *(koh-mah$^{(n)}$-say)* .... to begin, commence
comment *(koh-mah$^{(n)}$)* .... how
  Comment allez-vous? *(koh-moh$^{(n)}$)(tah-lay-voo)* ...
  .... How are you?
compagnie, la *(koh$^{(n)}$-pahn-yee)* .... company
compartiment, le *(koh$^{(n)}$-par-tuh-mah$^{(n)}$)* ..... compartment
complet, le *(koh$^{(n)}$-play)* .... suit (clothes)
comprendre *(koh$^{(n)}$-prah$^{(n)}$-druh)* .... to understand
compris (e) *(koh$^{(n)}$-pree)* .... included
concert, le *(koh$^{(n)}$-sair)* .... concert
concierge, le/la *(koh$^{(n)}$-see-airzh)* ... doorkeeper, concierge
confiture, la *(koh$^{(n)}$-fee-tewr)* .... jam
consigne, la *(koh$^{(n)}$-seen-yuh)* .... left-luggage office
continuer *(koh$^{(n)}$-tee-new-ay)* .... to continue
contravention, la *(koh$^{(n)}$-trah-vah$^{(n)}$-syoh$^{(n)}$)* .. parking ticket
conversation, la *(koh$^{(n)}$-vair-sah-syoh$^{(n)}$)* ..... conversation
corbeille à papier, la *(kor-bay)(ah)(pah-pee-ay)* .. wastebasket
correspondances, les *(koh-ray-spoh$^{(n)}$-dah$^{(n)}$s)* .. connections
costume de bain, le *(koh-stewm)(duh)(ba$^{(n)}$)* ...... swimsuit
côté, le *(koht)* .... side, coast
couchette, la *(koo-shet)* .... berth, bunk
couleur, la *(koo-luhr)* .... color
courrier, le *(koo-ree-ay)* .... mail
court (e) *(koor)* .... short
cousin, le *(koo-za$^{(n)}$)* .... cousin (male)
cousine, la *(koo-zeen)* .... cousin (female)
couteau, le *(koo-toh)* .... knife
coûter *(koo-tay)* .... to cost
coutume, la *(koo-tewm)* .... custom, habit
couverture, la *(koo-vair-tewr)* .... blanket
cravate, la *(krah-vaht)* .... necktie
crayon, le *(kray-yoh$^{(n)}$)* .... pencil
croissant, le *(kwah-sah$^{(n)}$)* .... crescent roll **109**

cuillère, la *(kwee-air)* . . . . spoon
cuisine, la *(kwee-zeen)* . . . . kitchen
cuisinière, la *(kwee-zeen-yair)* . . . . stove
cuit (e) *(kwee)* . . . . cooked
cuit au four *(kwee)(toh)(foor)* . . . . baked

D

dame, la *(dahm)* . . . . lady
dans *(dah⁽ⁿ⁾)* . . . . in, into
danse, la *(dah⁽ⁿ⁾s)* . . . . dance
d', de *(duh)* . . . . of, from, out of, some
de l', de la *(duh)(lah)* . . . . of, from, out of, some
de rien *(duh)(rya⁽ⁿ⁾)* . . . . you're welcome
décembre, le *(day-sah⁽ⁿ⁾m-bruh)* . . . . December
déclaration, la *(day-klah-rah-syoh⁽ⁿ⁾)* . . . . declaration
degré, le *(duh-gray)* . . . . degree
déjà *(day-zhah)* . . . . already
déjà vu *(day-zhah)(vew)* . . . . already seen
déjeuner, le *(day-zhuh-nay)* . . . . lunch
délicieux (délicieuse) *(day-lee-syuh)* . . . . delicious
demain *(duh-ma⁽ⁿ⁾)* . . . . tomorrow
demander *(duh-mah⁽ⁿ⁾-day)* . . . . . to ask, ask for
demi (e) *(duh-mee)* . . . . half
dentifrice, le *(dah⁽ⁿ⁾-tee-frees)* . . . . toothpaste
déodorant, le *(day-oh-doh-rah⁽ⁿ⁾)* . . . . deodorant
départ, le *(day-par)* . . . . departure
derrière *(dair-ee-air)* . . . . behind
des *(day)* . . . . some, from the
désir, le *(day-zeer)* . . . . desire
désoler *(day-zoh-lay)* . . . . to distress
je suis désolé *(zhuh)(swee)(day-zoh-lay)* . . . . . . I'm sorry
dessert, le *(day-sair)* . . . . dessert
deux *(duh)* . . . . two
deuxième *(duh-zee-em)* . . . . second
devant *(duh-vah⁽ⁿ⁾)* . . . . in front of
déviation, la *(day-vee-ah-syoh⁽ⁿ⁾)* . . . . detour
devoir *(duh-vwahr)* . . . . to have to, must
dictionnaire, le *(deek-syoh-nair)* . . . . dictionary
différent (e) *(dee-fay-rah⁽ⁿ⁾)* . . . . different
difficile *(dee-fee-seel)* . . . . difficult
dimanche, le *(dee-mah⁽ⁿ⁾sh)* . . . . Sunday
dîner, le *(dee-nay)* . . . . dinner
dire *(deer)* . . . . to say
direction, la *(dee-rek-syoh⁽ⁿ⁾)* . . . . direction
distance, la *(dee-stah⁽ⁿ⁾s)* . . . . distance
dit *(dee)* . . . . says
on dit *(oh⁽ⁿ⁾)(dee)* . . . . one says
dix *(deess)* . . . . ten
dix-huit *(deez-wheat)* . . . . eighteen
dix-neuf *(deez-nuf)* . . . . nineteen
dix-sept *(deez-set)* . . . . seventeen
docteur, le *(dohk-tur)* . . . . doctor
donc *(doh⁽ⁿ⁾k)* . . . . therefore
donnez-moi *(doh⁽ⁿ⁾-nay-mwah)* . . . . give me!
dormir *(dor-meer)* . . . . to sleep
douane, la *(doo-ah⁽ⁿ⁾)* . . . . customs
douche, la *(doosh)* . . . . shower
douze *(dooz)* . . . . twelve
drapeau, le *(drah-poh)* . . . . flag
droite *(dwaht)* . . . . right
du *(dew)* . . . . some, in the, from the

E

eau, la *(oh)* . . . . water
école, la *(ay-kohl)* . . . . school
économie, la *(ay-koh-noh-mee)* . . . . economy
110 Écosse, la *(ay-kohs)* . . . . Scotland

écrire *(ay-kreer)* . . . . to write
écrivez-moi *(ay-kree-vay-mwah)* . . . . write for me!
église, la *(ay-gleez)* . . . . church
elle *(el)* . . . . it, she
elles *(el)* . . . . they
en *(ah⁽ⁿ⁾)* . . . . in, to, into
en anglais *(ah⁽ⁿ⁾)(ah⁽ⁿ⁾-glay)* . . . . in English
en français *(ah⁽ⁿ⁾)(frah⁽ⁿ⁾-say)* . . . . in French
encore *(ah⁽ⁿ⁾-kor)* . . . . again, still, more
enfant, le *(ah⁽ⁿ⁾-fah⁽ⁿ⁾)* . . . . child
entre *(ah⁽ⁿ⁾-truh)* . . . . between
entrée, la *(ah⁽ⁿ⁾-tray)* . . . . entry
entrée principale, la *(ah⁽ⁿ⁾-tray)(pra⁽ⁿ⁾-see-pahl)* . . main entry
entrer *(ah⁽ⁿ⁾-tray)* . . . . to go in, enter
environ *(ah⁽ⁿ⁾-vee-roh⁽ⁿ⁾)* . . . . about
envoyer *(ah⁽ⁿ⁾-vwah-yay)* . . . . to send
épicerie, la *(ay-pee-suh-ree)* . . . . grocery store
escargot, le *(ess-kar-goh)* . . . . snail
Espagne, la *(eh-spahn-yuh)* . . . . Spain
espagnol (e) *(eh-spahn-yohl)* . . . . Spanish
est *(ay)* . . . . (it) is
est-ce *(ess)* . . . . is it, it is
est, le *(est)* . . . . east
et *(ay)* . . . . and
étage, le *(ay-tahzh)* . . . . floor, story
était *(ay-tay)* . . . . (it) was
état, le *(ay-tah)* . . . . state
États-Unis, les *(ay-tah-zoo-nee)* . . . . USA
été, le *(ay-tay)* . . . . summer
êtes *(et)* . . . . (you) are
étranger (étrangère) *(ay-trah⁽ⁿ⁾-zhay)* . . . . . foreign, abroad
être *(et-ruh)* . . . . to be
Europe, la *(uh-rohp)* . . . . Europe
européen (européenne) *(uh-roh-pay-yen)* . . . . . . European
excellent (e) *(ek-suh-lah⁽ⁿ⁾)* . . . . excellent
excusez-moi *(ek-skew-zay-mwah)* . . . . excuse me
exemple, le *(eg-zah⁽ⁿ⁾-pluh)* . . . . example
express, le *(ek-spress)* . . . . fast train
extrêmement *(ek-streh-muh-mah⁽ⁿ⁾)* . . . . . . extremely

F

facile *(fah-seel)* . . . . easy
faim, la *(fa⁽ⁿ⁾)* . . . . hunger
faire *(fair)* . . . . to do, make
fait *(fay)* . . . . (it) makes
faire la valise *(fair)(lah)(vah-leez)* . . . . to pack
famille, la *(fah-mee-yuh)* . . . . family
farci (e) *(far-see)* . . . . stuffed
fatigue, la *(fah-teeg)* . . . . fatigue, tiredness
fax, le *(fahx)* . . . . fax
femme, la *(fahm)* . . . . woman
fenêtre, la *(fuh-net-ruh)* . . . . window
fermé (e) *(fair-may)* . . . . closed
festival, le *(feh-stee-vahl)* . . . . festival
fête, la *(fet)* . . . . feast, festival
feu, le *(fuh)* . . . . fire
février, le *(fah-vree-ay)* . . . . February
fille, la *(fee-yuh)* . . . . girl, daughter
film, le *(feelm)* . . . . film
fils, le *(feess)* . . . . son
filtre, le *(feel-truh)* . . . . filter
fin, la *(fa⁽ⁿ⁾)* . . . . end
fleur, la *(fluhr)* . . . . flower
fleuriste, le *(fluhr-eest)* . . . . florist
foi, la *(fwah)* . . . . faith
fonctionnaire, le *(foh⁽ⁿ⁾-syoh⁽ⁿ⁾-nair)* . . functionary, civil servant
football, le *(foot-bahl)* . . . . soccer

forêt, la *(foh-ray)* . . . . forest
forme, la *(form)* . . . . form, shape
fourchette, la *(foor-shet)* . . . . fork
foyer, le *(fwah-yay)* . . . . home, hearth, lobby
frais (fraîche) *(fray)* . . . . fresh, cool
franc (franche) *(frah⁽ⁿ⁾)* . . . . frank, honest
franc, le *(frah⁽ⁿ⁾)* . . . . franc
français (e) *(frah⁽ⁿ⁾-say)* . . . . French
Français, les *(frah⁽ⁿ⁾-say)* . . . . the French people
France, la *(frah⁽ⁿ⁾s)* . . . . France
fréquence, la *(fray-kah⁽ⁿ⁾s)* . . . . frequency
frère, le *(frair)* . . . . brother
frit (e) *(free)* . . . . fried
froid (e) *(fwah)* . . . . cold
fromage, le *(froh-mahzh)* . . . . cheese
fruit, le *(fwee)* . . . . fruit
fruitier, le *(fwee-tee-ay)* . . . . fruit vendor
fumé *(few-may)* . . . . smoked
fumer *(few-may)* . . . . to smoke

G

galerie, la *(gah-leh-ree)* . . . . gallery, long room
gant, le *(gah⁽ⁿ⁾)* . . . . glove
garage, le *(gah-rahzh)* . . . . garage
garçon, le *(gar-soh⁽ⁿ⁾)* . . . . boy, waiter
gare, la *(gar)* . . . . train station
gâteau, le *(gah-toh)* . . . . cake
gauche *(gohsh)* . . . . left
généralement *(zhah-nay-rahl-mah⁽ⁿ⁾)* . . . . generally
géographie, la *(zhay-oh-grah-fee)* . . . . geography
gibier, le *(zhee-bee-ay)* . . . . wild game
glace, la *(glahs)* . . . . ice, ice cream
gomme, la *(gohm)* . . . . eraser
gourmand, le *(goor-mah⁽ⁿ⁾)* . . . . gourmand, glutton
gourmet, le *(goor-may)* . . . . gourmet
gouvernement, le *(goo-vair-nuh-mah⁽ⁿ⁾)* . . . . . . government
grand (e) *(grah⁽ⁿ⁾)* . . . . big, large, tall
grand-mère, la *(grah⁽ⁿ⁾-mair)* . . . . grandmother
grand-père, le *(grah⁽ⁿ⁾-pair)* . . . . grandfather
grands-parents, les *(grah⁽ⁿ⁾-pah-rah⁽ⁿ⁾)* . . . . . grandparents
grandeur, la *(grah⁽ⁿ⁾-dur)* . . . . greatness
grillé (e) *(gree-ay)* . . . . grilled
gris (e) *(gree)* . . . . gray
guichet, le *(ghee-shay)* . . . . counter, window
guide, le *(geed)* . . . . guide

H

habiter *(ah-bee-tay)* . . . . to live, reside
haut (e) *(oh)* . . . . high
en haut *(ah⁽ⁿ⁾)(oh)* . . . . above, upstairs
heure, la *(uhr)* . . . . hour
hier *(ee-air)* . . . . yesterday
hiver, le *(ee-vair)* . . . . winter
homme, le *(ohm)* . . . . man
horaire, le *(oh-rair)* . . . . timetable
horloge, la *(or-lohzh)* . . . . large clock
horlogerie, la *(or-loh-zhuh-ree)* . . . . watchmaker's shop
hors-d'oeuvre, le *(or-duh-vruh)* . . . . appetizers
hôtel, le *(oh-tel)* . . . . hotel
hôtelier, le *(oh-tel-yay)* . . . . hotelkeeper
huit *(wheat)* . . . . eight

I

ici *(ee-see)* . . . . here
idée, la *(ee-day)* . . . . idea
identification, la *(ee-dah⁽ⁿ⁾-tee-fee-kah-syoh⁽ⁿ⁾)* . . identification
il *(eel)* . . . . it, he

il faut *(eel)(foh)* . . . . it is necessary
il n'y a pas de quoi *(eel)(nyah)(pah)(duh)(kwah)* . . . .
. . *(eel)(nyah)(pah)(duh)(kwah)* . . you're welcome, it's nothing
il y a *(eel-yah)* . . . . there is, there are
île, la *(eel)* . . . . island
ils *(eel)* . . . . they
imperméable, le *(a⁽ⁿ⁾-pair-may-ah-bluh)* . . . . raincoat
importance, la *(a⁽ⁿ⁾-por-tah⁽ⁿ⁾s)* . . . . importance
important (e) *(a⁽ⁿ⁾-por-tah⁽ⁿ⁾)* . . . . important
impossible *(a⁽ⁿ⁾-poh-see-bluh)* . . . . impossible
inacceptable *(een-ahk-sep-tah-bluh)* . . . . unacceptable
industrie, la *(a⁽ⁿ⁾-dew-stree)* . . . . industry
information, la *(a⁽ⁿ⁾-for-mah-syoh⁽ⁿ⁾)* . . . . . . information
ingénieur, le *(a⁽ⁿ⁾-zhay-nyur)* . . . . engineer
inscription, la *(a⁽ⁿ⁾-skreep-syoh⁽ⁿ⁾)* . . . . inscription
instant, le *(a⁽ⁿ⁾-stah⁽ⁿ⁾)* . . . . moment, instant
institut, le *(a⁽ⁿ⁾-stee-tew)* . . . . institute
interdit (e) *(a⁽ⁿ⁾-tair-dee)* . . . . prohibited
intéressant (e) *(a⁽ⁿ⁾-tay-ruh-sah⁽ⁿ⁾)* . . . . interesting
intérieur, le *(a⁽ⁿ⁾-tay-ree-ur)* . . . . . . domestic, inside, interior
interurbain (e) *(a⁽ⁿ⁾-tair-ewr-ba⁽ⁿ⁾)* . . . . long-distance
Irlande, la *(eer-lahnd)* . . . . Ireland
Israël, le *(ees-rah-el)* . . . . Israel
Italie, la *(ee-tah-lee)* . . . . Italy
italien (italienne) *(ee-tah-lya⁽ⁿ⁾)* . . . . Italian

J - K

jambon, le *(zhah⁽ⁿ⁾-boh⁽ⁿ⁾)* . . . . ham
janvier, le *(zhah⁽ⁿ⁾-vee-ay)* . . . . January
Japon, le *(zhah-poh⁽ⁿ⁾)* . . . . Japan
japonais (e) *(zhah-poh-nay)* . . . . Japanese
jaquette, la *(zhah-ket)* . . . . woman's jacket
jardin, le *(zhar-da⁽ⁿ⁾)* . . . . garden
jaune *(zhohn)* . . . . yellow
je *(zhuh)* I
jeans, les *(jeans)* . . . . jeans
jeudi, le *(zhuh-dee)* . . . . Thursday
jeune *(zhun)* . . . . young
jour, le *(zhoor)* . . . . day
journal, le *(zhoor-nahl)* . . . . newspaper
juif (juive) *(zhweef)* . . . . Jewish
juillet, le *(zhwee-ay)* . . . . July
juin, le *(zhwa⁽ⁿ⁾)* . . . . June
jupe, la *(zhewp)* . . . . skirt
jus, le *(zhoo)* . . . . juice
juste *(zhoost)* . . . . just, fair, right
justice, la *(zhoo-stees)* . . . . justice
kilo, le *(kee-loh)* . . . . kilo
kilomètre, le *(kee-loh-meh-truh)* . . . . kilometer
kiosque, le *(kee-ohsk)* . . . . news-stand, kiosk

L

l', la *(lah)* . . . . the (singular)
lac, le *(lack)* . . . . lake
lait, le *(lay)* . . . . milk
laiterie, la *(lay-tuh-ree)* . . . . dairy
lampe, la *(lahmp)* . . . . lamp
langue, la *(lah⁽ⁿ⁾-gwuh)* . . . . language
lavabo, le *(lah-vah-boh)* . . . . washbasin
laver *(lah-vay)* . . . . to wash
le *(luh)* . . . . the (singular)
leçon, la *(luh-soh⁽ⁿ⁾)* . . . . lesson
lecture, la *(lek-tewr)* . . . . reading
légume, le *(lay-gewm)* . . . . vegetable
lent (e) *(lah⁽ⁿ⁾)* . . . . slow
lentement *(lah⁽ⁿ⁾-tuh-mah⁽ⁿ⁾)* . . . . slowly
les *(lay)* . . . . the (plural) **111**

lettre, la *(let-ruh)* . . . . letter
liberté, la *(lee-bair-tay)* . . . . liberty
librairie, la *(lee-brair-ree)* . . . . bookstore
libre *(lee-bruh)* . . . . free
lieu, le *(lyuh)* . . . . place
ligne, la *(leen-yuh)* . . . . line
limonade, la *(lee-moh-nahd)* . . . . lemonade
lire *(leer)* . . . . to read
liste, la *(leest)* . . . . list
lit, le *(lee)* . . . . bed
litre, le *(lee-truh)* . . . . liter
living-room, le *(lee-veeng-room)* . . . . living room
livre, le *(lee-vruh)* . . . . book
logement, le *(lohzh-mah⁽ⁿ⁾)* . . . . . . lodging, accommodation
long (longue) *(lohng)* . . . . long
louer *(loo-ay)* . . . . to rent
Louvre, le *(loo-vruh)* . . . . Louvre (museum)
lundi, le *(luh⁽ⁿ⁾-dee)* . . . . Monday
lunettes, les *(lew-net)* . . . . glasses
   lunettes de soleil, les *(lew-net)(duh)(soh-lay)* . . . sunglasses
Luxembourg, le *(lewk-sah⁽ⁿ⁾-boor)* . . . . Luxembourg

M

Madame *(mah-dahm)* . . . . Mrs.
Mademoiselle *(mahd-mwah-zel)* . . . . Miss
magasin, le *(mah-gah-za⁽ⁿ⁾)* . . . . store
   grand magasin, le *(grah⁽ⁿ⁾)(mah-gah-za⁽ⁿ⁾)* . . department store
magazine, le *(mah-gah-zeen)* . . . . magazine
magnifique *(mah-nee-feek)* . . . . magnificent
mai, le *(may)* . . . . May
maillot de bain, le *(my-oh)(duh)(ba⁽ⁿ⁾)* . . swimming trunks
maintenant *(ma⁽ⁿ⁾-tuh-nah⁽ⁿ⁾)* . . . . now
mais *(may)* . . . . but
maison, la *(may-zoh⁽ⁿ⁾)* . . . . house
mal *(mahl)* . . . . poorly, badly
malade *(mah-lahd)* . . . . sick
manger *(mah⁽ⁿ⁾-zhay)* . . . . to eat
manteau, le *(mah⁽ⁿ⁾-toh)* . . . . coat
marchand, le *(mar-shah⁽ⁿ⁾)* . . . . merchant
marché, le *(mar-shay)* . . . . market
mardi, le *(mar-dee)* . . . . Tuesday
mariage, le *(mah-ree-ahzh)* . . . . . . marriage, wedding
Maroc, le *(mah-rohk)* . . . . Morocco
marron *(mah-roh⁽ⁿ⁾)* . . . . brown
mars, le *(marss)* . . . . March
matin, le *(mah-ta⁽ⁿ⁾)* . . . . morning
mauvais (e) *(moh-vay)* . . . . bad
me *(muh)* . . . . to me
mécanicien, le *(may-kah-nee-sya⁽ⁿ⁾)* . . . . mechanic
médecin, le *(may-duh-sa⁽ⁿ⁾)* . . . . doctor
médicament, le *(may-dee-kah-mah⁽ⁿ⁾)* . . . . medicine
menu, le *(muh-new)* . . . . menu
mer, la *(mair)* . . . . sea
merci *(mair-see)* . . . . thank you
mercredi, le *(mair-kruh-dee)* . . . . Wednesday
mère, la *(mair)* . . . . mother
messieurs, les *(mes-syur)* . . . . gentlemen
mètre, le *(meh-truh)* . . . . meter
métro, le *(may-troh)* . . . . subway
midi, le *(mee-dee)* . . . . noon
mille *(meel)* . . . . one thousand
minuit, le *(mee-nwee)* . . . . midnight
minute, la *(mee-newt)* . . . . minute
minuterie, la *(mee-new-tuh-ree)* . . . . automatic light switch
miroir, le *(mir-wahr)* . . . . mirror
mode, la *(mohd)* . . . . fashion
   à la mode *(ah)(lah)(mohd)* . . . . fashionable

moins *(mwa⁽ⁿ⁾)* . . . . less
   moins le quart *(mwa⁽ⁿ⁾)(luh)(kar)* . . . . a quarter to
mois, le *(mwah)* . . . . month
moment, le *(moh-mah⁽ⁿ⁾)* . . . . moment
mon *(moh⁽ⁿ⁾)* . . . . my
monde, le *(mohnd)* . . . . world
   tout le monde *(too)(luh)(mohnd)* . . . . everyone
monnaie, la *(moh-nay)* . . . . coins, money
Monsieur *(muh-syuh)* . . . . Mr.
montagne, la *(moh⁽ⁿ⁾-tahn-yuh)* . . . . mountain
montrer *(moh⁽ⁿ⁾-tray)* . . . . to show
mot, le *(moh)* . . . . word
motocyclette, la *(moh-toh-see-klet)* . . . . motorcycle
mots croisés, les *(moh)(kwah-zay)* . . . . . . crossword puzzle
mouchoir, le *(moo-shwahr)* . . . . handkerchief
mousse, la *(moos)* . . . . whipped cream, froth
moutarde, la *(moo-tard)* . . . . mustard
mouton, le *(moo-toh⁽ⁿ⁾)* . . . . mutton
multicolore *(mewl-tee-koh-lor)* . . . . . . multi-colored
musée, le *(mew-zay)* . . . . museum
musique, la *(mew-zeek)* . . . . music
musulman (e) *(mew-zewl-mah⁽ⁿ⁾)* . . . . Moslem

N

nation, la *(nah-syoh⁽ⁿ⁾)* . . . . nation
nature, la *(nah-tewr)* . . . . nature
naturel (naturelle) *(nah-tew-rel)* . . . . natural
ne . . . pas, n'. . . pas *(nuh)(pah)* . . . . no, not
ne . . . rien *(nuh)(rya⁽ⁿ⁾)* . . . . nothing
nécessaire *(nay-seh-sair)* . . . . necessary
nécessité, la *(nay-seh-see-tay)* . . . . necessity
neige (il neige) *(nehzh)* . . . . snow (it snows)
nettoyage à sec, le *(neh-twah-yahzh)(ah)(sek)* . . dry cleaner's
neuf *(nuf)* . . . . nine
neuf (neuve) *(nuf)* . . . . new
noir (e) *(nwahr)* . . . . black
nom, le *(noh⁽ⁿ⁾)* . . . . name
nombre, le *(nohm-bruh)* . . . . number
non *(noh⁽ⁿ⁾)* . . . . no
nord, le *(nor)* . . . . north
note, la *(noht)* . . . . bill in a hotel
notre *(noh-truh)* . . . . our
nous *(noo)* . . . . we
nouveau (nouvelle) *(noo-voh)* . . . . new
novembre, le *(noh-vah⁽ⁿ⁾m-bruh)* . . . . November
nuit, la *(nwee)* . . . . night
numéro, le *(noo-may-roh)* . . . . number

O

objet, le *(ohb-zhay)* . . . . object
obligatoire *(oh-blee-gah-twahr)* . . . . . compulsory, obligatory
observation, la *(ohb-sair-vah-syoh⁽ⁿ⁾)* . . . . observation
occupation, la *(oh-kew-pah-syoh⁽ⁿ⁾)* . . . . occupation
occupé (e) *(oh-kew-pay)* . . . . busy, occupied
octobre, le *(ohk-toh-bruh)* . . . . October
odeur, la *(oh-dur)* . . . . smell
oeufs, les *(uh)* . . . . eggs
   oeuf à la coque *(uh)(ah)(lah)(kohk)* . . . . boiled egg
   oeufs brouillés *(uh)(broo-yay)* . . . . scrambled eggs
officiel (officielle) *(oh-fee-syel)* . . . . official
omelette, la *(ohm-let)* . . . . omelette
omnibus, le *(ohm-nee-boos)* . . . . slow train
on *(oh⁽ⁿ⁾)* . . . . one, people, they, we
   on fait ça *(oh⁽ⁿ⁾)(fay)(sah)* . . . . one does that
oncle, le *(oh⁽ⁿ⁾-kluh)* . . . . uncle
ont *(oh⁽ⁿ⁾)* . . . . (they) have
onze *(oh⁽ⁿ⁾z)* . . . . eleven

opéra, le *(oh-peh-rah)* .... opera
optimiste, le *(ohp-tee-meest)* .... optimist
orange, la *(oh-rah⁽ⁿ⁾zh)* .... orange (color)
orchestre, le *(or-kess-truh)* .... orchestra
ordinaire *(or-dee-nair)* .... ordinary
ordinateur, le *(or-dee-nah-tur)* .... computer
oreiller, le *(oh-ray-yay)* .... pillow
organisé (e) *(or-gah-nee-zay)* .... organized
Orient, le *(oh-ree-ah⁽ⁿ⁾)* .... Orient
original (e) *(oh-ree-zhee-nahl)* .... original
origine, la *(oh-ree-zheen)* .... origin
ou *(oo)* .... or
où *(oo)* .... where
oublier *(oo-blee-ay)* .... to forget
ouest, le *(west)* .... west
oui *(wee)* .... yes
ouvert (e) *(oo-vair)* .... open
ouvrez *(oo-vray)* .... open!

P

page, la *(pahzh)* .... page
pain, le *(pa⁽ⁿ⁾)* .... bread
paire, la *(pair)* .... pair
pantalon, le *(pah⁽ⁿ⁾-tah-loh⁽ⁿ⁾)* .... trousers
pantoufle, la *(pah⁽ⁿ⁾-too-fluh)* .... slipper
Pape, le *(pahp)* .... Pope
papeterie, la *(pah-peh-tuh-ree)* .... stationery store
papier, le *(pah-pee-ay)* .... paper
paquet, le *(pah-kay)* .... package
par *(par)* .... by, per
par avion *(par)(ah-vyoh⁽ⁿ⁾)* .... by airmail
parapluie, le *(pah-rah-plew-ee)* .... umbrella
parc, le *(park)* .... park
pardon *(par-doh⁽ⁿ⁾)* .... excuse me
parent, le *(pah-rah⁽ⁿ⁾)* .... parent, relative
parfait (e) *(par-fay)* .... perfect
parfum, le *(par-fuh⁽ⁿ⁾)* .... perfume
parfumerie, la *(par-few-muh-ree)* .... perfumery
parking, le *(par-keeng)* .... parking lot
parler *(par-lay)* .... to speak
partir *(par-teer)* .... to leave, depart
passeport, le *(pahs-por)* .... passport
pâtisserie, la *(pah-tee-suh-ree)* .... pastry, pastry shop
pauvre *(poh-vruh)* .... poor
payer *(pay-yay)* .... to pay
Pays-Bas, les *(pay-ee-bah)* .... Netherlands
peigne, le *(pen-yuh)* .... comb
pellicule, la *(peh-lee-kewl)* .... film
pendule, la *(pah⁽ⁿ⁾-dewl)* .... clock
perdre *(pair-druh)* .... to lose
père, le *(pair)* .... father
personne, la *(pair-sohn)* .... person
petit (e) *(puh-tee)* .... small
petit-déjeuner, le *(puh-tee-day-zhuh-nay)* ...... breakfast
peu *(puh)* .... a little
peuple, le *(puh-pluh)* .... people
pharmacie, la *(far-mah-see)* .... pharmacy
photo, la *(foh-toh)* .... photo, photograph
phrase, la *(frahz)* .... sentence
pièce, la *(pyess)* .... room, piece
pilule, la *(pee-lewl)* .... pill
pique-nique, le *(peek-neek)* .... picnic
placard, le *(plah-kar)* .... cupboard, closet
place, la *(plahs)* .... seat, place, square (in a town)
plaisir, le *(play-zeer)* .... pleasure
avec plaisir *(avek)(play-zeer)* .... with pleasure
plan, le *(plah⁽ⁿ⁾)* .... map

plat du jour, le *(plah)(dew)(zhoor)* .... daily special
pleut (il pleut) *(pluh)* .... rain (it rains)
plus *(plew)* .... more
poisson, le *(pwah-soh⁽ⁿ⁾)* .... fish
poissonnerie, la *(pwah-soh⁽ⁿ⁾-nuh-ree)* .... fish shop
poivre, le *(pwah-vruh)* .... pepper
Pôle nord, le *(pohl)(nor)* .... North Pole
Pôle sud, le *(pohl)(sood)* .... South Pole
police, la *(poh-lees)* .... police
politesse, la *(poh-lee-tess)* .... politeness
politique, la *(poh-lee-teek)* .... politics
pomme, la *(pohm)* .... apple
pont, le *(poh⁽ⁿ⁾)* .... bridge
porc, le *(por)* .... pork
port, le *(por)* .... port
porte, la *(port)* .... door, gate
portefeuille, le *(port-fuh-yuh)* .... wallet
porteur, le *(por-tur)* .... porter
Portugal, le *(por-too-gahl)* .... Portugal
poste, la *(pohst)* .... mail
poste de police, le *(pohst)(duh)(poh-lees)* .... police station
potage, le *(poh-tahzh)* .... soup
poulet, le *(poo-lay)* .... chicken
pour *(poor)* .... for
pourboire, le *(poor-bwahr)* .... tip
pourquoi *(poor-kwah)* .... why
pousser *(poo-say)* .... to push
pouvoir *(poo-vwahr)* .... to be able to, can
premier (première) *(pruh-mee-air)* .... first
prendre *(prah⁽ⁿ⁾-druh)* .... to take
préposition, la *(pray-poh-zee-syoh⁽ⁿ⁾)* .... preposition
président, le *(pray-zee-dah⁽ⁿ⁾)* .... president
presse, la *(press)* .... press, media
printemps, le *(prah⁽ⁿ⁾-tah⁽ⁿ⁾)* .... spring
prix, le *(pree)* .... price
problème, le *(proh-blem)* .... problem
programme, la *(proh-grahm)* .... program
propre *(proh-pruh)* .... clean
protestant (e) *(proh-teh-stah⁽ⁿ⁾)* .... Protestant
pyjama, le *(pee-zhah-mah)* .... pajamas

Q

qu' *(kuh)* .... what, that
Qu'est-ce que c'est? *(kess)(kuh)(say)* .... What is it?
quai, le *(kay)* .... platform
quand *(kah⁽ⁿ⁾)* .... when
quarante *(kah-rah⁽ⁿ⁾t)* .... forty
quart, le *(kar)* .... a quarter
et quart *(ay)(kar)* .... a quarter past
quartier, le *(kar-tee-ay)* .... quarter, district
quatorze *(kah-torz)* .... fourteen
quatre *(kah-truh)* .... four
quatre-vingt-dix *(kah-truh-va⁽ⁿ⁾-deess)* .... ninety
quatre-vingts *(kah-truh-va⁽ⁿ⁾)* .... eighty
que *(kuh)* .... what, that
Québec *(kay-bek)* .... Quebec (Canada)
quel *(kel)* .... what, which
quelle *(kel)* .... what, which
question, la *(kes-tyoh⁽ⁿ⁾)* .... question
qui *(key)* .... who, what
quinze *(ka⁽ⁿ⁾z)* .... fifteen
quoi *(kwah)* .... what

R

raisin, le *(ray-za⁽ⁿ⁾)* .... grape
raisin sec, le *(ray-za⁽ⁿ⁾)(sek)* .... raisin
rapide *(rah-peed)* .... fast   **113**

rapide, le *(rah-peed)* . . . . (fast) train
rasoir, le *(rah-zwahr)* . . . . razor
recette, la *(ruh-set)* . . . . recipe, receipt
récréation, la *(ray-kray-ah-syoh[n])* . . . . recreation
réfrigérateur, le *(ray-free-zhay-rah-tuhr)* . . . . . refrigerator
région, la *(ray-zhoh[n])* . . . . region, area
religion, la *(ruh-lee-zhoh[n])* . . . . religion
Renaissance, la *(ruh-nay-sah[n]s)* . . rebirth, the Renaissance
rendez-vous, le *(rah[n]-day-voo)* . . . . date, appointment
repas, le *(ruh-pah)* . . . . meal
répéter *(ray-pay-tay)* . . . . to repeat
répétez *(ray-pay-tay)* . . . . repeat!
réponse, la *(ray-poh[n]s)* . . . . answer
république, la *(ray-pew-bleek)* . . . . republic
RER *(air-uh-air)* . . . . transportation network (in Paris)
réservation, la *(ray-zair-vah-syoh[n])* . . . . reservation
réserver *(ray-zair-vay)* . . . . to reserve, to book
résidence, la *(ray-zee-dah[n]s)* . . . . residence
résistance, la *(ray-zee-stah[n]s)* . . . . resistance
restaurant, le *(reh-stoh-rah[n])* . . . . restaurant
reste, le *(rehst)* . . . . rest, remaining
rester *(reh-stay)* . . . . to remain, stay
réveil, le *(ray-vay)* . . . . alarm clock
révolution, la *(ray-voh-lew-syoh[n])* . . . . revolution
revue, la *(ruh-vew)* . . . . magazine
rez-de-chaussée, le *(ray-duh-shoh-say)* . . . . ground floor
riche *(reesh)* . . . . rich
rideau, le *(ree-doh)* . . . . curtain
rien *(rya[n])* . . . . nothing
robe, la *(rohb)* . . . . dress
robe de chambre, la *(rohb)(duh)(shah[n]-bruh)* . . . . bathrobe
rose *(rohz)* . . . . pink
rôti (e) *(roh-tee)* . . . . roasted
rouge *(roozh)* . . . . red
route, la *(root)* . . . . highway, road
rue, la *(rew)* . . . . street
russe *(roos)* . . . . Russian
Russie, la *(roo-see)* . . . . Russia

S

sac, le *(sack)* . . . . bag, sack
sac à main, le *(sahk)(ah)(mah[n])* . . . . handbag
sacré *(sah-kray)* . . . . sacred
sage *(sahzh)* . . . . wise, well-behaved
saison, la *(say-zoh[n])* . . . . season
salade, la *(sah-lahd)* . . . . salad
salle à manger, la *(sahl)(ah)(mah[n]-zhay)* . . . . dining room
salle d'attente, la *(sahl)(dah-tah[n]t)* . . . . waiting room
salle de bain, la *(sahl)(duh)(ba[n])* . . . . bathroom
salon, le *(sah-loh[n])* . . . . living room
salut *(sah-lew)* . . . . hello, hi
salutation, la *(sah-lew-tah-syoh[n])* . . . . greeting
samedi, le *(sahm-dee)* . . . . Saturday
sandale, la *(sah[n]-dahl)* . . . . sandal
sandwich, le *(sah[n]-dweech)* . . . . sandwich
sans *(sah[n])* . . . . without
santé, la *(sah[n]-tay)* . . . . health
en bonne santé *(ah[n])(bun)(sah[n]-tay)* . . . . healthy
sauce, la *(sohs)* . . . . sauce
saumon, le *(soh-moh[n])* . . . . salmon
savoir *(sah-vwahr)* . . . . to know (a fact)
savon, le *(sah-voh[n])* . . . . soap
science, la *(see-ah[n]s)* . . . . science
second (e) *(suh-goh[n]d)* . . . . second
second, la *(seh-goh[n]d)* . . . . second (time)
secours, le *(suh-koor)* . . . . help
114 au secours *(oh)(suh-koor)* . . . . help!

secrétaire, le/la *(suh-kray-tair)* . . . . secretary
sécurité, la *(say-kew-ree-tay)* . . . . security
seize *(sehz)* . . . . sixteen
sel, le *(sel)* . . . . salt
semaine, la *(suh-men)* . . . . week
sentiment, le *(sah[n]-tee-mah[n])* . . . . feeling
sept *(set)* . . . . seven
septembre, le *(sep-tah[n]m-bruh)* . . . . September
serveur, le *(sair-vur)* . . . . waiter
serveuse, la *(sair-vuz)* . . . . waitress
service, le *(sair-vees)* . . . . service
serviette, la *(sair-vyet)* . . . . napkin, towel
short, le *(short)* . . . . shorts
s'il vous plaît *(seel)(voo)(play)* . . . . please
similarité, la *(see-mee-lar-ee-tay)* . . . . similarity
situation, la *(see-tew-ah-syoh[n])* . . . . situation
six *(seess)* . . . . six
ski, le *(skee)* . . . . skiing
ski-nautique, le *(skee-noh-teek)* . . . . water skiing
slip, le *(sleep)* . . . . underpants
soeur, la *(suhr)* . . . . sister
soif, la *(swahf)* . . . . thirst
soir, le *(swahr)* . . . . evening
soixante *(swah-sah[n]t)* . . . . sixty
soixante-dix *(swah-sah[n]t-deess)* . . . . seventy
soleil, le *(soh-lay)* . . . . sun
somme, la *(sohm)* . . . . sum
sont *(soh[n])* . . . . (they) are
Sorbonne, la *(sor-bun)* . . . . part of University of Paris
sortie, la *(sor-tee)* . . . . exit
sortir *(sor-teer)* . . . . to go out, leave, exit
soupe, la *(soup)* . . . . soup
sous *(soo)* . . . . under
sous-sol, le *(soo-sohl)* . . . . basement
soutien-gorge, le *(soo-tya[n]-gorzh)* . . . . brassiere
souvenir, le *(soo-vuh-neer)* . . . . souvenir
spectacle, le *(spek-tah-kluh)* . . . . . . spectacle, performance
sport, le *(spor)* . . . . sport
station d'essence, la *(stah-syoh[n])(day-sah[n]s)* . . gas station
station de métro, la *(stah-syoh[n])(duh)(may-troh)* . . . .
. . . . subway station
stop, le *(stohp)* . . . . stop
stopper *(stoh-pay)* . . . . to stop
stupide *(stew-peed)* . . . . stupid
stylo, le *(stee-loh)* . . . . pen
sucre, le *(soo-kruh)* . . . . sugar
sud, le *(sood)* . . . . south
Suède, la *(swed)* . . . . Sweden
suis *(swee)* . . . . (I) am
Suisse, la *(swees)* . . . . Switzerland
suivant (e) *(swee-vah[n])* . . . . following
supérieur (e) *(syoo-pay-ree-ur)* . . . . superior, upper
supermarché, le *(soo-pair-mar-shay)* . . . . . . supermarket
sur *(sewr)* . . . . on
sûr (e) *(sur)* . . . . sure, certain
surprise, la *(sewr-preez)* . . . . surprise
sympathique *(sa[n]-pah-teek)* . . . . likeable, nice
système, le *(see-stem)* . . . . system

T

tabac, le *(tah-bah)* . . . . tobacco
table, la *(tah-bluh)* . . . . table
tableau, le *(tah-bloh)* . . . . picture
taille, la *(tie)* . . . . size (clothing)
tante, la *(taunt)* . . . . aunt
tapis, le *(tah-pee)* . . . . carpet
tapisserie, la *(tah-pee-suh-ree)* . . . . tapestry, wallpaper

tarif, le *(tah-reef)* . . . . tariff, fare
tasse, la *(tahs)* . . . . cup
taxe, la *(tahx)* . . . . tax, charge
taxi, le *(tahx-ee)* . . . . taxi
teeshirt, le *(tee-shirt)* . . . . T-shirt
télécarte, la *(tay-lay-kart)* . . . . telephone card
télégramme, le *(tay-lay-grahm)* . . . . telegram
téléphone, le *(tay-lay-fohn)* . . . . telephone
téléphoner *(tay-lay-foh-nay)* . . . . to telephone
téléphoniste, le *(tay-lay-foh-neest)* . . . . operator
téléviseur, le *(tay-lay-vee-zur)* . . . . . . television set
température, la *(tah(n)-pay-rah-tewr)* . . . . temperature
temps, le *(tah(n))* . . . . weather, time
tennis, le *(teh-nees)* . . . . tennis
terrasse, la *(tay-rahs)* . . . . terrace, sidewalk (café)
thé, le *(tay)* . . . . tea
théâtre, le *(tay-ah-truh)* . . . . theater
thermal (e) *(tair-mahl)* . . . . thermal
thermomètre, le *(tair-moh-meh-truh)* . . . . thermometer
ticket, le *(tee-kay)* . . . . ticket
timbre-poste, le *(ta(n)-bruh-pohst)* . . . . stamp
tirer *(tee-ray)* . . . . to pull
toilettes, les *(twah-let)* . . . . toilets
toujours *(too-zhoor)* . . . . always
tour, la *(tour)* . . . . tower
tour, le *(tour)* . . . . tour, circumference
tourner *(toor-nay)* . . . . to turn
tout *(too)* . . . . everything
tout droit *(too)(dwah)* . . . . straight ahead
train, le *(tra(n))* . . . . train
transport, le *(trah(n)-spor)* . . . . transportation
treize *(trehz)* . . . . thirteen
trente *(trah(n)t)* . . . . thirty
très *(treh)* . . . . very
tricolore *(tree-koh-lor)* . . . . tricolored
tricot de peau, le *(tree-koh)(duh)(poh)* . . . . undershirt
trois *(twah)* . . . . three
troisième *(twah-zee-em)* . . . . third
trop cher *(troh)(shair)* . . . . too expensive
trouver *(troo-vay)* . . . . to find
tu *(too)* . . . . you (singular/informal)
Tunisie, la *(tew-nee-zee)* . . . . Tunisia
typique *(tee-peek)* . . . . typical

U

un *(uh(n))* . . . . a, one (masculine)
une *(ewn)* . . . . a, one (feminine)
unique *(ew-neek)* . . . . sole, only, single
universel *(ew-nee-vair-sel)* . . . . universal
université, la *(ew-nee-vair-see-tay)* . . . . university
urgence, la *(ewr-zhah(n)s)* . . . . urgency, emergency
utilisez *(oo-tee-lee-zay)* . . . . use!

V

vacances, les *(vah-kah(n)s)* . . . . vacation, holiday
vais *(vay)* . . . . (I) go
valise, la *(vah-leez)* . . . . suitcase
valse, la *(vahls)* . . . . waltz
vanille, la *(vah-nee-yuh)* . . . . vanilla
variété, la *(vah-ree-ay-tay)* . . . . variety
veau, le *(voh)* . . . . veal
veine, la *(ven)* . . . . vein (in the body)
vendre *(vah(n)-druh)* . . . . to sell
vendredi *(vah(n)-druh-dee)* . . . . Friday
venir *(vuh-neer)* . . . . to come
vent, le *(vah(n))* . . . . wind
vente, la *(vah(n)t)* . . . . sale

verbe, le *(vairb)* . . . . verb
verre, le *(vair)* . . . . glass
verre à vin, le *(vair)(ah)(va(n))* . . . . wine glass
version, la *(vair-syoh(n))* . . . . version
vert (e) *(vair)* . . . . green
veston, le *(veh-stoh(n))* . . . . jacket, blazer
vêtement, le *(vet-mah(n))* . . . . clothes
viande, la *(vee-ah(n)d)* . . . . meat
vie, la *(vee)* . . . . life
vierge, la *(vee-airzh)* . . . . virgin
vieux (vieille) *(vee-yuh)* . . . . old
vigne, la *(veen-yuh)* . . . . grape vine
vigneron, le *(veen-yur-oh(n))* . . . . wine-grower
vignoble, le *(veen-yoh-bluh)* . . . . vineyard
village, le *(vee-lahzh)* . . . . village
ville, la *(vee)* . . . . city
vin, le *(va(n))* . . . . wine
vingt *(va(n))* . . . . twenty
violet (violette) *(vee-oh-lay)* . . . . violet
visite, la *(vee-zeet)* . . . . visit
visiter *(vee-zee-tay)* . . . . to visit
vitamine, la *(vee-tah-meen)* . . . . vitamin
vite *(veet)* . . . . fast
vocabulaire, le *(voh-kah-bew-lair)* . . . . vocabulary
voilà *(vwah-lah)* . . . . there is, there are
voir *(vwahr)* . . . . to see
voiture, la *(vwah-tewr)* . . . . car
voiture à louer, la *(vwah-tewr)(ah)(loo-ay)* . . . . rental car
vol, le *(vohl)* . . . . flight
volaille, la *(voh-lie)* . . . . poultry
vos *(voh)* . . . . your
votre *(voh-truh)* . . . . your
vouloir *(voo-lwahr)* . . . . to want
je voudrais *(zhuh)(voo-dray)* . . . . I would like
vous *(voo)* . . . . you (singular and plural)
vous *(voo)* . . . . to you
voyage, le *(vwah-yahzh)* . . . . trip, travel
Bon voyage! *(boh(n))(vwah-yahzh)* . . . . . . have a good trip
voyager *(vwah-yah-zhay)* . . . . to travel
voyager en avion *(vwah-yah-zhay)(ah(n))(ah-vyoh(n))* . . to fly
voyageur, le *(vwah-yah-zhur)* . . . . traveler

W - Y - Z

W.C., le *(doo-bul-vay-say)* . . . . water closet, toilet
wagon, le *(vah-goh(n))* . . . . railroad car
wagon-lit, le *(vah-goh(n)-lee)* . . . . sleeping car
wagon-restaurant, le *(vah-goh(n)-reh-stoh-rah(n))* . . dining car
week-end, le *(week-end)* . . . . weekend
western, le *(wes-tairn)* . . . . western (film)
whisky, le *(wee-skee)* . . . . whisky
y a-t-il *(yah-teel)* . . . . are there? is there?
zèbre, le *(zeh-bruh)* . . . . zebra
zèle, le *(zel)* . . . . zeal, ardor
zénith, le *(zay-neet)* . . . . zenith, peak
zéphyr, le *(zay-feer)* . . . . balmy breeze
zéro *(zay-roh)* . . . . zero
zodiaque, le *(zoh-dee-ahk)* . . . . zodiac
zone, la *(zohn)* . . . . zone
zone de silence, la *(zohn)(duh)(see-lah(n)s)* . . . . quiet zone
zoo, le *(zoh)* . . . . zoo
zoologie, la *(zoh-oh-loh-zhee)* . . . . zoology
zut! *(zewt)* . . . . rats! darn!

Did you have fun learning your new language?
We at Bilingual Books hope you enjoy your
travels wherever they might take you, and
don't forget your Pocket Pal™!

This beverage guide is intended to explain the variety of beverages available to you while **en France ou** any other French-speaking country. It is by no means complete. Some of the experimenting has been left up to you, but this should get you started.

BOISSONS CHAUDES (hot drinks)

café noir	coffee, black
café au lait	coffee with milk
café crème	coffee with cream
café express	espresso
café filtre	filtered coffee

chocolat	cocoa
thé	tea
thé au citron	tea with lemon
thé au lait	tea with milk

BOISSONS FROIDES (cold drinks)

lait froid	cold milk
lait aromatisé	flavored milk
eau minérale	mineral water
jus de fruits	fruit juice
jus d'orange	orange juice
jus de pomme	apple juice
jus de tomate	tomato juice
orange pressée	fresh squeezed orange juice
thé glacé	iced tea
café glacé	iced coffee
glace	ice

BIÈRES (beer) There are a variety of brands including both **blonde** (light) and **brune** (dark). **La bière** is purchased **en bouteille** (bottle) or **à la pression** (draught).

VINS (wine) Wine production in France is closely controlled by the government, making it much easier to know what you are buying. You may drink wine by the **verre** (glass), the **carafe** (carafe) or the **bouteille** (bottle).

vin rouge	red wine
vin blanc	white wine
vin rosé	rosé wine
vin mousseux	sparkling wine
vin ordinaire	table wine
vin de table	table wine
vin de la maison	the "house" wine
vin du pays	local wine of the region

A.O.C. (Appellation d'origine contrôlée)
   superior wine
V.D.Q.S. (Vins délimités de qualité supérieure)
   choice wine
Premier cru/Grand cru
   good vintage wine

APÉRITIFS (aperitifs) These may be enjoyed straight or over ice.

porto	port
Pastis	aniseed-flavored aperitif
Pineau des Charentes	grape juice and cognac
Kir	Crème de Cassis and white wine

ALCOOL (spirits) Cocktail drinking is not widespread in France. The following are available in large, international hotels and "**Bars américains.**"

gin	gin
vodka	vodka
rhum	rum
whisky	scotch
bourbon	bourbon
martini dry	American maritini

La Carte
menu

Préparation (preparation)

cuit	cooked
cru	raw
rôti	roasted
frit	fried
cuit au four	baked
grillé	grilled
farci	stuffed or filled
bouilli	boiled
fumé	smoked
mariné	marinated
braisé	braised
en croûte	cooked in pastry crust
gratiné	sprinkled with cheese
au jus	cooked in its own juice
bleu	extremely rare
saignant	rare
à point	medium rare
bien cuit	well done

Autres (others)

confiture	jam
miel	honey
huile	oil
vinaigre	vinegar
moutarde	mustard
riz	rice
nouilles	noodles
pâtes	pasta
fromage	cheese
gâteau	cake
pâtisserie	pastry
glace	ice cream
chantilly	whipped cream
yaourt	yoghurt

FOLD HERE

Pommes de terre (potatoes)

croquettes	mashed, breaded and fried
gratin dauphinois	scalloped
frites	French-fried
à l'anglaise	peeled and boiled
nature	plain boiled
maître d'hôtel	boiled and sautéed
purée	mashed
vapeur	steamed

Fruit (fruit)

pomme	apple
poire	pear
abricot	apricot
pêche	peach
banane	banana
orange	orange
mandarine	mandarin orange
cerise	cherry
prune	plum
pruneau	prune
melon	melon
pamplemousse	grapefruit
pastèque	watermelon
raisin	grape
raisin sec	raisin
grenade	pomegranate
ananas	pineapple
citron	lemon
compote de fruits	stewed fruits

Baies (berries)

fraise	strawberry
framboise	raspberry
mûre	blackberry
cassis	black currant
myrtille	bilberry
airelle	blueberry
groseille	red currant

(boh⁽ⁿ⁾) *(nah-pay-tee)*

Bon appétit!
enjoy your meal

FOLD HERE

Salades (salads)

laitue	lettuce salad
chicorée	chicory
escarole	coarse-leafed green lettuce
endive belge	Belgian endive
mâche	wild field lettuce
romaine	romaine
mimosa	green salad with egg yolks
mixte	mixed
niçoise	string beans, potatoes, and tuna
verte	tossed green
de saison	seasonal
de tomates	tomato
vinaigrette	in vinegar and oil

Légumes (vegetables)

haricots verts	green string beans
flageolets	small, pale green beans
petits pois	peas
lentilles	lentils
asperges	asparagus
carottes	carrots
épinards	spinach
poireaux	leeks
tomates	tomatoes
champignons	cultivated mushrooms
chanterelles	wild mushrooms
morilles	morel, wild mushrooms
chou	cabbage
chou-fleur	cauliflower
choux de Bruxelles	brussels sprouts
betteraves	beets
maïs	corn
concombres	cucumbers
navets	turnips
oignons	onions
radis	radishes
ail	garlic
artichauts	artichoke
aubergines	eggplant
courgettes	zucchini squash

Viande (meat)

Veau (veal)

blanquette de veau	veal stew with gravy
côte de veau	veal chop
côtelette de veau	veal chop
foie de veau	calf's liver
fricassée de veau	veal stew
médaillons de veau	medallions of pan-fried veal
noisette de veau	tenderloin morsels of veal
poitrine de veau farcie	stuffed breast of veal
ris de veau	veal sweetbreads
rognons de veau	veal kidneys
tendron de veau	braised breast of veal
tête de veau	head of veal
escalope de veau	veal cutlet

Agneau (lamb)

carré d'agneau	lamb rib roast
côte/côtelette	lamb chop
épaule d'agneau	lamb shoulder
gigot d'agneau	leg of lamb

Volaille (poultry)

poulet	chicken
coq au vin	chicken in wine sauce
canard	duck
caneton	duckling
chapon	capon
caille	quail
oie	goose
faisan	pheasant
dinde	turkey

Gibier (wild game)

gigue de chevreuil	roast leg of venison
bécasse	woodcock
escalope de sanglier	cutlets of wild boar
cuissot de marcassin	roast leg of wild pig
râble de lapin	saddle of rabbit

Boeuf (beef)

boeuf bourguignon	red wine stew
carbonades de boeuf	sautéed and braised slices
côte de boeuf	beef rib steaks
entrecôte de boeuf	boneless beef rib steak
estouffade de boeuf	braised beef in wine stew
filet de boeuf	tenderloin of beef
médaillon de boeuf	thick discs of tenderloin
queue de boeuf	oxtail
tournedos	beef tenderloin
terrine de boeuf	casserole stew
tripes	stomach lining
moelle	beef bone marrow

Porc (pork)

côte/côtelette	pork chop
carré de porc provençal	rib loin roast with spices
cuissot de porc	fresh ham roast
jarret de porc	pork shank
pied de porc	pig's foot
rognons de porc	pork kidneys
rôti de porc	pork roast

Poissons et fruits de mer (fish and seafood)

anchois	anchovies
anguille	eel
cabillaud	codfish
calamar	squid
carpe	carp
colin	hake
coquillages	shellfish
coquilles Saint-Jacques	scallops
crabe	crab
crevettes	shrimps
écrevisses	fresh-water crayfish
flétan	halibut
grenouille	frog
hareng	herring
homard	lobster, with claws
langouste	spiny lobster, no claws
langoustine	shellfish
moules	mussels
perche	perch
poulpe	small octopus
saumon	salmon
sole	sole
truite	trout
thon	tuna

Hors-d'oeuvre (appetizers)

huîtres	oysters
assiette de charcuterie	assorted sausages, salamis
crudités	raw vegetables
escargots	snails
foie gras truffé	goose liver with truffles
jambon cru	raw-cured ham
pâté de campagne	country style, course pâté
salade panachée	mixed vegetable salad
terrine maison	house pâté in terrine
croque-monsieur	grilled ham and cheese sandwich
croque-madame	grilled chicken and cheese sandwich

Potages (soups)

bisque	cream soup with seafood
bouillabaisse	rich fish soup
crème de tomates	cream of tomato
pistou	vegetable soup
soupe du jour	soup of the day
soupe à l'oignon	onion soup
consommé	clarified stock
soupe à la reine	chicken soup with rice
velouté de légumes	thick vegetable soup
vichyssoise	potato and leek soup

Oeufs (eggs)

à la coque	soft-boiled
mollets	medium-boiled
brouillés	scrambled
durs	hard-boiled
pochés	poached
omelette nature	plain omelette
omelette au fromage	cheese omelette
quiche	cheese and egg pie

FOLD HERE
FOLD HERE

Learn _another_ language ... in just 10 minutes a day ®

More than 2,000,000 people around the world have learned a language the _10 minutes a day_® way and had fun doing it!

Available in ten languages!

You can e-mail us at: info@ bilingualbooks.org

To order call

1-800-488-5068
1-206-340-4422
or
Complete the order form and mail it with payment to:

Bilingual Books, Inc.
511 Eastlake Ave. E.
Seattle, WA 98109
USA

Le bon de commande
order form

To Place Your Order

☎ Call **1-800-488-5068** today or Cut out this form and send with payment to:

✉ Bilingual Books, Inc.
511 Eastlake Avenue E.
Seattle, WA 98109 USA

Title	Qty.	Price/book	Total
Chinese		US $17.95	
French		US $17.95	
German		US $17.95	
Hebrew		US $17.95	
Inglés		US $17.95	
Italian		US $17.95	
Japanese		US $17.95	
Norwegian		US $17.95	
Russian		US $19.95	
Spanish		US $17.95	
		Subtotal	$
		Shipping*	+
		WA residents add tax	+
		Total Order	$

Check Shipping Prices Below!

Please Check:

❏ Bill my credit card account ❏ Visa ❏ MC

No. _____

Exp. date _____

Signature _____

❏ My check for $ _____ is enclosed.

Name _____

Address _____

City _____ State ____ Zip _____

Telephone No. (_____) _____

* SHIPPING PRICES (all prices in US dollars)

In the United States add $5 for the first item (book or cassettes) and $1 for each additional item. On foreign orders add $9 for the first item and $5 for each additional item for airmail shipment.

All prices subject to change without notice.

Now that you've finished...

You've done it!

You've completed all the Steps, stuck your labels, flashed your cards, clipped your menu and pocketed your Pal™. Do you realize how far you've come and how much you've learned? You've accomplished what it could take years to achieve in a traditional language class.

You can now confidently

- ask questions,
- understand directions,
- make reservations,
- order food and
- shop anywhere.

And you can do it all in a foreign language! You can now go anywhere — from a large cosmopolitan restaurant to a small, out-of-the-way village where no one speaks English. Your experiences will be much more enjoyable and worry-free now that you speak the language and know something of the culture.

Yes, learning a foreign language can be fun. And no, not everyone abroad speaks English.

Kristine Kershul

Have a wonderful time, whether your trip is to Europe, Asia or simply across the border.